"Mary Ann has always been a passionate writer who tugs on the heartstrings of women just like her, and once again she has prepared us well for the next stage of life in *When You're Facing the Empty Nest*."

—Pam Farrel
Author, *10 Best Decisions a Woman Can Make*

☆☆☆

"I wish this book had been written fifteen years go! Careful preparation is the key to negotiating most life changes, Mary Ann Forehlich writes, yet how many of us planned ahead for the empty nest? A wealth of encouragement for the woman whose sense of identity walked out the door with her last child, as well as wise advice for the young mother not yet aware that she will not always be the hub of her children's lives."

—Lawana Blackwell
Author, *A Table by the Window*,
Gresham Chronicles series, Tales of London series

☆☆☆

Books by

Mary Ann Froehlich

What's a Smart Woman Like You Doing in a Place Like This?

Music Education in the Christian Home

An Early Journey Home: Helping Families Work Through the Loss of a Child

Music Therapy with Hospitalized Children: A Creative Arts Child Life Approach

*Holding Down the Fort: Help and Encouragement for Wives Whose Husbands Travel**

*What to Do When You Don't Know What to Say**

*What to Do When You Don't Know What to Say to Your Own Family**

101 Ideas for Piano Group Class: Building an Inclusive Music Community for Students of All Ages and Abilities

Nurturing the WRITE Relationship: Developing the Family Writing Lifestyle

When You're Facing the Empty Nest

*Books coauthored with PeggySue Wells

When You're Facing the Empty Nest

Mary Ann Froehlich

BETHANY HOUSE PUBLISHERS
Minneapolis, Minnesota

Cover design by Andrea Nelson

Published by Bethany House Publishers
11400 Hampshire Avenue South
Bloomington, Minnesota 55438

Bethany House Publishers is a division of
Baker Publishing Group, Grand Rapids, Michigan.

Printed in the United States of America

Library of Congress Cataloging-in-Publication Data

Froehlich, Mary Ann, 1955-
When you're facing the empty nest : avoiding midlife meltdown when your child leaves home / by Mary Ann Froehlich.
p. cm.
Summary: "Ideal for women whose children are graduating from high school, this sensitive book lets readers know they aren't alone in their feelings of loss. It offers a sense of hope for the future and practical suggestions for parenting their young adult children. Includes discussion questions for use in small groups"—Provided by publisher.
ISBN 0-7642-0018-6 (pbk.)
1. Empty nesters—Religious life. 2. Mothers—Religious life. I. Title.

BV4527.4.F76 2005
248.8'431—dc22

2005004801

Dedication

Dedicated to my children, husband, and parents,
who "gave me something to say"
and to my amazing midlife support network.

Acknowledgments

With many thanks to:

—Ann Parrish and the team at Bethany House
who brought this vision to completion.
—the midlife women who graciously shared
their lives with me and have been my inspiration.

About the Author

Mary Ann Froehlich, DMA, CCLS, MT-BC, is a board-certified music therapist and a Suzuki music teacher, specializing in teaching children with special needs. She is a contributor to journals and an author of ten books. In addition, her piano/harp arrangements are published as the *Collages* series. Mary Ann has worked in hospitals, schools, churches, and private practice. She has graduate degrees in piano and harp performance and music education/music therapy, with a doctorate from the University of Southern California. As a certified Child Life specialist, she has worked with hospitalized children and has an MA degree in theology/pastoral care from Fuller Theological Seminary. Mary Ann and her husband have been married for twenty-seven years, and she is the midlife mom of two college-age daughters and a teenage son.

Contents

Introduction: Welcome to Midlife

"How would you describe your experience when your children left for college?" I asked my friend.

"Oh, that's easy. When one of my children leaves home, it's like having another limb cut off."

Facing the empty nest season of life is one of the greatest challenges for women. As our children leave home, we also experience changes in our bodies, a midlife evaluation of our vocation and purpose, jolting constant reminders in our culture's media that we look middle-aged, and relational changes with our spouses and parents. Many of us may lose friends to cancer. Life seems to be changing in every direction.

Careful preparation is the key to negotiating most life changes. We invest time in preparing for major events, such as marriage, a new job, a move, or having a baby. We certainly prepare our children to leave home, through college prep programs, SAT seminars, guiding them through the college application process, purchasing supplies for dorm rooms, and much more. Yet we do not prepare ourselves for when they actually leave.

I wrote this book because I was unprepared for the emotional roller coaster of entering the empty nest/midlife experience. Very few women openly discuss it, and no one plainly laid out for me how difficult it would be. I encountered books on midlife topics, with titles such as *How to Be a Happy Empty Nest Mom*. Giving such a book to a mother whose child has recently left home would be like giving a book entitled *You Can Be a Happy Widow* to a woman whose husband died last week.

If you are finding the empty nest changes in your life to be harder than expected, I want you to know that you are not alone. Every woman struggles. Some just have more effective coping methods than others. I realized I needed to grieve first. Then I began observing, talking to, and reading about how other women had handled their midlife challenges. You will read their stories in the *Midlife Glimpses* sections between chapters. These examples are as varied as the individual women they represent. I invite you to immerse yourself in the broad spectrum of midlife experiences. There is no one way to experience this transition. (Names have often been changed to protect the privacy of these women.)

This interactive book is intended to help you walk through the process of facing the empty nest. Questions for journaling or discussion are included at the end of each chapter. This book can be read alone, but ideally it would be used with a supportive friend or small group. Quotes that have inspired me and biblical verses that have comforted me are also included.

Most of us attended nine months of prenatal appointments and childbirth classes, anticipating the birth of our newborn. Preparation for the empty nest is also necessary. Consider this book your final childbirth class. You are completing what you started almost twenty years ago—it's time for the final stage of labor and delivery.

Chapter 1
Grieving When Your Child Leaves Home

When one of my children leaves home, it's like having another limb cut off . . .

Amputation? That reaction sounded a little extreme . . . until my firstborn left for college. At first I thought I was going crazy. My sadness seemed entirely out of proportion for such a normal, expected event as my daughter's departure for college. After all, didn't our daughter's blossoming independence mean that we as parents had done our job?

I kept telling myself, "This is ridiculous. Certainly no one has died." Yet I had to admit that a piece of me actually had died—the piece that daily interacted with my daughter. I was faced with reminders of my loss throughout each day: the empty chair at the dinner table; running to my daughter's bedroom to tell her the latest news and finding it unoccupied and quiet; reaching for her favorite foods at the market and then lowering my hand, as the tears welled. I felt foolish sharing this with anyone. My husband was not falling apart, and I had other children at home who needed my attention. From my observations, no one else was as traumatized as I was. I felt silly and very much alone.

I not only missed my daughter, I missed her life—her

myriad of friends coming in and out of the house, discussing their joys and latest crises with me. I missed hearing her play the piano in the evenings. I was unprepared for the silence. (My mother recently shared with me how she missed listening to my piano practices after I left for college. I did not understand her pain when I was a college freshman, but I understand it now.) An entire chapter of my life had closed overnight. I would no longer daily parent my daughter.

Having worked with terminally ill children and their families, I recognized that I was walking through the classic stages of grief; however, there had been no wake or closure ceremony, no flowers, no sympathy cards, no bereavement support groups, no acknowledgment. My life was radically changing and no one seemed to notice.

I couldn't just pick up the phone and hear my daughter's voice—beyond her voice mail message—whenever I desired. She was immersed in a new life, always on the run, attending classes and multiple university activities, bonding with people I had never met. Our chats were short and sweet. I was thrilled that she had adapted so quickly to her new lifestyle. Yet how would I adapt to the void in mine?

The alternatives were not any better. My friend's son was lonely and homesick at college, calling her twice daily. She carried double misery, hers and his. Another friend's daughter was not accepted to any of the colleges she hoped to attend, and remained at home while her friends left for their respective campuses. Others I knew had adult children still living at home, unable to financially support themselves. Some of our friends were raising grandchildren, a common phenomenon today. They experienced an even deeper grief.

It's a Process

The empty nest is not a chronological event or stage. It is a process, as individual as you are, a necessary weaning process.

Depending on whether you had children earlier or later in life—and how many children you have—you may be anywhere from your late thirties to your fifties when your last child leaves home. Some women are grandmothers by this time.

Though my experience is with children leaving for college, young adults leave home for multiple reasons, such as entering the military or moving out of the house to start a job and become independent. Our pain as parents is the same. Some young people leave home because of conflicts and remain estranged from their families. I would never claim to understand the depth of their anguish; I can only imagine it.

Weaning is a complicated process. Some mothers are baffled when the child they had always been so close to is suddenly angry and rebellious before leaving home. The more connected children are to parents, sometimes the harder they must work to break away, which is confusing for any mom and dad. Escalating conflicts are common as moving day approaches. Our emotions are raw, but we do not know how to share them. An emotional argument is easier for some families to handle than a tearful, prolonged good-bye.

Some mothers breeze through the empty nest transition. After the initial adjustment, they find that they love their new life and enjoy having more free time. Other mothers count the days until their children return home for a vacation break, and then spend the day after they leave crying, grieving for them all over again.

Even though we may be unprepared for the shock when our first child leaves, our role still remains intact if we have younger children living at home. But as each child leaves, "another limb is cut off." And when our youngest child leaves, we lose our daily identity as a mom. Sending an only child into the world (instant empty nest) is probably the most painful experience for parents.

Your Job is Done

One of the most helpful reality checks I received was through my daughter's university. As part of the summer orientation weekend, we parents attended a group counseling session led by staff psychologists. They began the seminar by playing a recording describing a young boy leaving for his first day of kindergarten, and soon we were all in tears. One mother shouted from the back of the room, "Now why did you do that?! You don't think I'm already struggling enough?" We wanted to applaud that angry mom. Yet we parents needed to cry (apart from our children) and face the stark reality of what was happening in our lives.

On the final day of orientation, all the parents were treated to an elegant luncheon. In the midst of the meal, our university host came to the microphone and said, "Now I need to tell you that at this very moment, your children are registering for their fall classes. I know that every parent in this room wants to leave immediately and go help their child. But you won't. Your job is done. It's their turn. If they don't learn to do this without you now, they'll never learn." He was right. Every parent in that room wanted to give some final advice to his/her child.

One more piece of advice . . . one more hug . . . *one more.* Be prepared that one of the hardest things you will experience in life is that final good-bye at an airport or the first time you walk away from your child's dorm room or apartment, leaving him or her behind. Mothers have been known to sob for the entire length of the trip home—whether it be thirty minutes or ten hours. It's at that moment we realize we are the ones being left behind.

Beginning Steps to Letting Go

Step #1

Allow yourself to grieve. Cry. Mourn the loss of a daily relationship with your child. You are not going crazy. You are not the only one who has experienced this parting.

Imagine how parents felt in the 1800s as their pioneer children traveled west, unsure if they would see them again. The Atlantic Ocean was once called the "Bowl of Tears" because of all the parents that were saying a final farewell to their children who were settling in new lands.

Accept the fact that you will experience a major "letdown." Make few demands of yourself. You participated in every step of preparing your child to leave home, from helping with the application process, making college visits, encouraging your child in selecting a school, purchasing dorm room needs, attending orientation, and more. Yet now your child is starting a new life and you are returning to your old one, with one big difference—your child's absence. You feel left out of the fun and excitement of starting a new adventure.

Step #2

The goal now is developing friendships and a mutual support system with your adult children. Your first job is done, but your next one is beginning. The truth is that you haven't lost anything or anyone, but it will feel misplaced for a while.

Comfort from God's Word

The heart knows its own grief best,
nor can a stranger share its joy.
PROVERBS 14:10

Yahweh is near to the brokenhearted,
he helps those whose spirit is crushed.
PSALM 34:18

You have noted my agitation,
now collect my tears in your wineskin!
Then my enemies will have to fall back
as soon as I call for help.
This I know: that God is on my side.

PSALM 56:8–9

Save me, O God:
For the waters have risen up to my neck.
I sink in muddy depths and have no foothold;
I am swept into deep water, and the flood carries me away.
I am wearied with crying out, my throat is sore,
my eyes grow dim as I wait for God to help me.

PSALM 69:1–3

THE NEW ENGLISH BIBLE

Blessed are those who mourn, for they will be comforted.

MATTHEW 5:4

Near the cross of Jesus stood his mother, his mother's sister, Mary the wife of Clopas, and Mary Magdalene. When Jesus saw his mother there, and the disciple whom he loved standing nearby, he said to his mother, "Dear woman, here is your son," and to the disciple, "Here is your mother." From that time on, this disciple took her into his home.

JOHN 19:25–27

Imagine how Mary felt when she walked away from her son at the cross. In the midst of His torturous death, Jesus understood His mother's pain.

Questions
for Journaling or Discussion

1. Where are you in your empty nest transition? Has your firstborn or your youngest child left home? Are you at the beginning, in the middle, or at the end of the process?

2. Have you allowed yourself to grieve? Healthy grief work requires time. Some mothers are paralyzed with grief when a child leaves home; others take the changes reasonably in stride. Where are you on the continuum?

3. Read Psalm 77:1–6 in addition to reviewing the preceding verses. I call Psalm 77 the "Griever's Psalm." Respond to 77:5–6:

My thoughts went back to times long past,
I remembered forgotten years;
all night long I was in deep distress,
as I lay thinking, my spirit was sunk in despair.

THE NEW ENGLISH BIBLE

4. If possible, talk with your own mother about your departure from home. To give you some perspective, compare her feelings with your feelings as a young person.

5. What do you miss most about your child? Late night chats? Helping with homework? Cooking you son's favorite foods? Going to the movies or shopping with your daughter? The chaos of teenagers coming in and out of your home? Be specific. Write a letter to your child that you will never send.

6. Reality check: What do you *not* miss? Emotional explosions? Anger? Arguing about curfew? Money conflicts? Unexpected hysteria? A messy bedroom? Be honest.

A mother is someone who lives with her heart outside her body.

Unknown

Put your head on the chest of God and weep.

Nicole Johnson

When a mother is left, the lone hub of a wheel, with no other lives revolving around her, she faces a total re-orientation. It takes time to re-find the center of gravity.

Anne Morrow Lindbergh

Midlife Glimpses

Liz thought that she had handled her firstborn daughter's departure for college in another state unusually well, until the first day of school arrived for the rest of her children. She made the rounds of her children's bedrooms, waking each for breakfast. On autopilot, Liz entered her oldest daughter's room last to wake her and was startled by the empty bed. She suddenly realized that she would never wake her daughter up for school again and help her start the day. At that moment, she began to grieve.

Stacey's life revolved around her son. She could not imagine life after her only child left home. She refused to think about it. After her son left for college across the country, she went to bed and cried for days, sinking into a deep depression. Too late she realized that her identity was completely wrapped up in being the mother of her superstar son. Her husband was finally able to convince Stacey to seek professional help, and she began a slow recovery, finding new purpose in life.

When their last child left home, Angela and her husband sold their home, purchased a beautiful piece of property, and left to travel throughout Europe for three months. Their college-age children met them at different points in their journey. When Angela and her husband returned home, they began building their dream house.

Teri and her husband were lonely after their children left for college. Never one to sit idle, Teri applied for a promotion and received it. She entered graduate school to pursue a doctorate. She took up tennis and also began daily training and walking in marathons around the country. She colored her hair blond and invested in braces. She never looked better. Since neither of her children could host a twenty-fifth wedding anniversary party for their parents because of distance, Teri planned it herself and invited her closest friends and relatives to celebrate the start of a new season of life. Their children took flights home to surprise them at the celebration.

Debbie and her husband found raising their sons to be the most meaningful experience of their lives. After their sons left home, they felt their empty nest home was too quiet. Debbie and her husband took in a three-year-old foster child, with plans to adopt her.

Lynn's husband had always traveled for his family business while their children were growing up. When their children left for college, Lynn was happy to be free to travel with her husband on his business trips. Soon she accepted a prominent position in his company.

As a mother of three adult children, two in college, Verdell Davis became a widow. Her husband and three close friends were returning from a Focus on the Family men's retreat when they died in a plane crash. Verdell had been a pastor's wife for twenty-seven years, sharing his ministries. She and her husband married young and she had never lived alone. Out of her pain she wrote the book *Riches Stored in Secret Places.*

Kathy wishes that she could experience the empty nest stage. She and her husband are financially supporting their adult children, who live at home, as well as raising a grandchild. Friends and church members are quick to offer advice about tough love. Kathy wishes they would walk in her shoes, understanding how complicated it is to have a relationship with adult children who struggle with serious problems, especially when a young child is involved.

~

Maria was a widow at age thirty-six. Two years later she remarried and conceived a child. At age fifty-five Maria was thrilled to be sending her only daughter off to college. She did not understand why other parents were not as happy. Maria had immigrated to this country when she married her first husband, a professor in the United States, and wanted her daughter to have the opportunities that Maria never had. She had saved her money to provide for her daughter's education at a prestigious college. She felt that her daughter's new life was a dream come true for both of them.

~

After her last child left for college, Rachel began taking foster children into her home. Her foster agency contact soon learned that Rachel was especially gifted at helping abused children. Rachel offered these children a loving, stable home while they were recovering from abuse.

~

A special bond is formed between a mother and daughter when they are in the midst of planning a wedding. Ann thoroughly enjoyed sharing the preparations with her daughter, Amy. They were in constant communication as the wedding day approached. The ceremony and reception went as planned and Ann celebrated giving her daughter a lovely wedding day. Then she realized the mission that had kept them so close had been accomplished. More difficult than grieving her daughter's departure for college, Ann now faced a new layer of the letting-go process. The marriage of children is a final, healthy break from their families. Today Ann is enjoying relating to Amy "wife to wife."

Chapter 2
Midlife Meltdown ... or Masterpiece?

There are three responses to crisis: coping, creating, and transforming.

—Pat Gaudette and Gay Courter

I met Lisa at a Christian music conference. She wanted me to write some articles for her creative arts organization. I invited her to my home later in the month to discuss it. I was in my midtwenties with a two-year-old daughter. Lisa was in her late forties. As we began talking, my daughter approached me to ask a question. Lisa sternly told her to leave us alone. Then Lisa proceeded to tell me that she had just left her husband and three children. She explained that she had sacrificed everything to take care of them, and now it was her turn to live as she pleased.

Then Lisa made the statement I have never forgotten: "Don't give up your life and dreams for your family. You think this will never happen to you, but it will. Just give it twenty years." With that warning, Lisa actually got into a bright red convertible and drove off. I had naïvely thought that the midlife crisis was a myth until that day. I never heard from Lisa again, but I took this stranger's warning to heart.

Through the years, I would think about her visit and wonder what I could do to avoid having a midlife meltdown. Today I am in my late forties with three children. Thanks to Lisa, this transition did not take me by surprise.

My husband had a similar experience in his late twenties. An older mentor told him that the midlife crisis was a reality. He said, "But it doesn't have to be a crisis if you prepare for it. It can be an event, a wonderful, positive event. Don't avoid thinking about it. Plan for it."

My husband and I had both been warned.

The Crisis of Change

The Chinese characters for "crisis" have a twofold definition. They can be interpreted to mean either "danger" or "opportunity." A crisis is a danger that threatens to overwhelm an individual or a family. A crisis is also defined as a turning point for better or worse, an opportunity for positive change. Common to every crisis is the experience of *change.*

A crisis can blindside you, sabotaging your life, or it can provide a magical opportunity to pursue adventures and dreams never imagined. The good news is that you have a choice. You can choose to have a midlife meltdown or create a midlife masterpiece.

You can choose to give up or you can choose to trust and follow God. View this season in your life as an opportunity to devour God's Word. The Bible is an entire book about people facing crisis and change—about people who run toward God or walk away from Him in the midst of crisis. Following God is always the best choice. It is the safest choice, although it feels anything *but* safe in the chaos of change. Yes, the choice to follow Him will often involve hard work. But by midlife, we should know that anything worthwhile and valuable usually requires hard work.

Vulnerable Midlife

The French refer to the midlife season as *demón de midi,* "the devil who invades the noonday of life." C. S. Lewis wrote that the midlife years were excellent campaigning weather for the devil. Why are we unusually vulnerable during our middle-age years? One of the primary reasons is that we realize time is running out. We face our own mortality. Thinking "someday I will do that" is no longer workable and we panic. The German term for midlife is *Torschlusspanik,* which means "closed-door panic" or "to be worried that one has missed the boat." All of a sudden we realize that if we don't reach for those unrealized dreams now, it will be too late. We have peaked in our careers. Often our jobs and relationships have lost their sparkle or their stability; the adrenaline rush is gone.

Yet this doesn't have to be a painful revelation. We evaluate our past successes and failures as well as future opportunities. The midlife season forces us to reevaluate our lives. In her book *Passages,* Gail Sheehy calls this the "bonus stage."

Most midlife travelers enter a dark place when they realize that some of their youthful dreams are realistically not going to happen. The more dreams we had as young people or the closer we were to achieving those goals, the more frustrated we are as midlife men and women. We do not grieve over pipe dreams. We grieve the loss of true opportunities, like the star athlete who was on his way to a major-league career but was derailed because of an injury or the accomplished dancer who could not enter a major ballet company because of an unexpected pregnancy.

Sometimes we place our dreams on our children's shoulders, wanting to give them the opportunities we didn't have. Often that weight is too much for our children. We view their lives so full of possibilities and potential. We are happy for our children yet saddened that while their opportunities are exploding, ours are narrowing. We hunger to have all those possibilities ahead of us again. We watch our children spread their wings to leave the nest, while our wings may feel clipped.

Unfortunately, the feeling that one has settled for less is

why affairs are prevalent in midlife, even for Christian men and women. They want to find the love of their life or their soul mate before it is too late, thinking that another human being is what has been missing. Reevaluation of one's life can be done in constructive as well as destructive ways.

Cleaning Out Old Wounds

One of the most painful yet healthiest challenges of midlife is that we can no longer ignore issues that we have placed for years on the back burner. Our emotional baggage simply becomes too heavy to carry. We must clean out old wounds. We must face unresolved issues with parents, spouses, children, siblings, or friends. As one woman explained to her midlife husband who was leaving her, "Even if you leave me, you will need to resolve your painful issues. Facing your wounds is similar to lancing a boil. Initially you will be in more pain, but once it is cleaned out, you will be able to fully heal and recover."

When my husband was a freshman in high school, his father and only brother were killed in a lake accident. His life changed in a moment, leaving his grieving mother to raise him alone. As a thirteen-year-old boy, my husband could not effectively grieve, so he immersed himself in nonstop activities to numb the pain. Still running at breakneck speed, he reached his forties not understanding why anger so often consumed him. He was having a midlife meltdown. He finally needed to grieve for his father and brother, and it was long, hard, painful work. He had to clean out the anger of a thirteen-year-old boy who had suddenly lost the center of his world—his dad. It is common for people who have lost a parent early in life to face their grief when they reach the age at which their parent died. They are like a time bomb.

Victims of childhood abuse are also among those who are usually not ready to fully face that nightmare until midlife.

Whether abused emotionally, physically, verbally, or sexually, midlife men and women can no longer bury their pain and begin to understand the toll it has taken on their lives. Seeking professional help is an important step toward healing.

Richard Rhodes waited until midlife to write *A Hole in the World* about his childhood abuse. He states that many life experiences cannot be written about or effectively shared with others until midlife, because we do not have the perspective needed to face them. One of the gifts of midlife is wisdom.

The Sandwich Generation

During the midlife years is when most of us lose our parents—our anchor. Just when we have lived through our own parenting challenges and appreciate our parents' role in our lives, our time with them is shortened. We realize that our parents were our age when they were raising us. They experienced their own pain and problems. Compassion begins to replace any resentment we harbor for mistakes our parents made. We know that we are not perfect parents either. As one woman said, "Just as my relationship with my mom and dad was healing, they died during the same year. I'm forty-five years old and feel like an orphan." I've also known this sorrow in my midlife years. My beloved father went into the hospital for an angiogram, the next day had open-heart surgery, and the following day died in intensive care. We are losing our children from our homes and our parents from our lives. Some of us lose our parents to death, while others lose parents to dementia and other mental diseases (a double loss).

Midlife men and women have been called the "sandwich generation," as they finish caring for adolescent children only to start taking care of ailing parents. Instead of driving children to baseball games, dance lessons, and music rehearsals, we are driving our parents and other aging relatives to medical appointments. Judith Viorst in *Necessary Losses* explains:

> *In midlife, we discover that we are destined to become our parents' parents. Few of us factored this into our life's plans. As responsible adults we try to do the best we can, though we liked it better being our children's parents. But, as we are finding—with exceedingly mixed emotions—that's ending too. For our children are gradually leaving, leaving for other houses and cities, for other countries. They are living beyond our control and beyond our care.*[1]

We have barely survived navigating life with angry teens who are trying to figure out their independence, and now we are helping parents who are frustrated and angry about losing their independence.

Our marriages are often strained as we try to cope with the changes. We feel adrift. These stressors are called triggers. Depending on the number of triggers occurring simultaneously, our meltdown can be mild or severe. For example, Stacey's midlife experience went from mild to emotional paralysis in six months. Her only son left to attend college across the country, her mother died, and her job was eliminated due to downsizing at work. Each of these would have been difficult experiences, but the combination was disastrous.

A New Challenge

The midlife transition is a relatively new challenge. In the early 1900s, parents died an average of eighteen months after their children moved out of the home. Midlife was short and retirement was almost nonexistent. Today the baby boomers who are hitting midlife comprise 30 percent of the population.

As Christian women, we can face our midlife transition, knowing we have a remarkable opportunity to live out our faith in front of observers. It won't be easy. Our perspective should be radically different from the world's perspective. We can revel in the fact that our faith collides with our culture at every turn. Whether the issue is external appearance, mortality, commitment to marriage, purpose, or caring for growing children or parents, we can base our lives on biblical truth, not cultural opinion.

In art and design classes, we learn that the most important element in any room is the focal point. Walking into a room, our attention can be held by a beautiful painting, fireplace, sculpture, or artistic floral arrangement. If the focal point works, everything else in the room revolves around it and makes sense. Flaws recede into the background. Jesus Christ is our focal point. When we keep our eyes glued to Him, everything else will recede into the background.

Encouragement from God's Word

Trust wholeheartedly in Yahweh,
put no faith in your own perception;
in every course you take, have him in mind:
he will see that your paths are smooth.
PROVERBS 3:5–6

Man's heart makes the plans,
Yahweh gives the answer.
PROVERBS 16:1

I know the plans I have in mind for you—it is Yahweh who speaks—plans for peace, not disaster, reserving a future full of hope for you. Then when you call to me, and come to plead with me, I will listen to you. When you seek me, you shall find me, when you seek me with all your heart; I will let you find me.

JEREMIAH 29:11–14A

Questions for Journaling or Discussion

1. Have you experienced a "closed-door panic" in midlife? Do you have unrealized dreams? Explain.

2. What are your old wounds? Are you feeling the need to face unresolved issues in your life?

3. Describe yourself as part of the "sandwich generation." What challenges do you face with your parents and other aging relatives?

4. List each change you have experienced this year. Do you have few or multiple stressors/triggers?

5. Review Jeremiah 29:11–14a. How often have you heard verse 11 quoted about trusting God with our future? Yet verses 13–14 are critical: *When you seek me, you shall find me, when you seek me with all your heart; I will let you find me.* How can you seek God with all your heart?

God knows how to lead us to the point of crisis, and He knows how to lead us through it . . . . There is no way out but God.

L. B. Cowman

After thirty years or more of floundering around and screwing up, you will finally know, and when you get serious you will be dealing with the one thing you've been avoiding all along—your wounds. This is very painful.

Anne Lamott

The evidence is in and you are the verdict.

Anne Lamott

Midlife Glimpses

Stephanie described herself as a career mom. She found motherhood to be a multi-faceted, creative career, with a little bit of everything. She helped direct stage productions. She conducted parenting seminars. Stephanie could not imagine finding a job more fulfilling than motherhood. Stephanie's father died shortly after her first child left for college. She entered a black pit of despair.

Karen had lived through the departure of three children for college, but nothing prepared her for saying good-bye to her adult son as he joined the military and left to serve in Iraq. She followed the news reports closely, praying that her son was not one of the casualties of battle. Every time her son was scheduled to return home on furlough, his tour of duty was extended. Karen often awoke in the middle of the night with the realization that her son was fighting across the world at that moment.

Denise did not expect to spend her empty nest years caring for her mother. She tries to balance daily visits to her mother, who has Alzheimer's, with being available to her husband and grown children, which often seems an impossible task. Most painful is the fact that Denise's mother rarely recognizes her.

Linda's two sons were away at college and her younger daughter was in her final years in high school, when her oldest son's new wife was diagnosed with multiple sclerosis. Her son and his wife also had an infant son. As the wife's condition deteriorated, Linda became more involved in caring for her grandson. She and her husband raised him, as his mother was placed in a nursing care facility for years before dying.

With two teenage boys at home and a daughter preparing to leave for college in another state, Christine discovered that she had unknowingly delayed her empty nest stage for twenty years. She was pregnant. Her shock was softened by her family's excitement and the camaraderie of two friends, also in their midforties, who were expecting babies. One friend, whose son had left for college, was expecting twins. As Christine's older children left home, she and her husband had the challenge of raising an only child, one with learning disorders. A few people mistook them for grandparents. Their son's friends' parents were twenty years younger than they. In addition to raising their young son, Christine and her husband embarked on a second adventure, moving to an idyllic community near the ocean. They had hoped to someday retire to a seaside town. Her husband's job promotion made that dream an early reality. They have found their unexpected midlife changes to far surpass their imagined future.

Chapter 3
The Botox Age

Are you just growing old . . . or are you also growing up?
—Charles Swindoll

In this season of loss, not only are our children leaving home, but our bodies are also changing. We are losing our youthful appearance, energy, agility, and sometimes our health. We are experiencing perimenopause or menopause. Doctor appointments start becoming a regular part of our schedules.

We are bombarded with cultural messages that leave no doubt in our minds that reaching midlife is considered unattractive, sometimes even unacceptable. Looking younger today is big business. Daily we see magazine ads, television commercials, and reality makeover shows telling us that we can reverse the aging process. I feel like that mother shouting from the back of the room at my daughter's college orientation, "Don't you think I'm already struggling enough?"

The American Society of Plastic Surgeons states that plastic surgery procedures have quadrupled in the past ten years. In our parents' generation, movie stars and celebrities underwent plastic surgery, often in secret. With the new technology of today, our own friends are having face-lifts, tummy tucks, laser surgery, botox or collagen injections, teeth whitening, liposuction, breast enhancement, and other treatments. This brings an entirely different kind of pressure to bear on midlife women. Not only are some women trying to look younger, they are trying to look better than when they were young.

I have always contended that we can be at our ideal body weight, but we cannot change our genetic proportions. Yet today people are changing their proportions. Resculpting a body and removing flaws are possible. Physical perfection is attainable. Plastic surgery addiction is an actual phenomenon as people strive for the perfect body. Plastic surgeons treat just as many male patients as female. Hair transplants are especially popular for men.

If these procedures were all inexpensive and pain free, what aging man or woman would not opt for some improvements?

Poison for Our Souls

When asked if her business was suffering because of the economy, one spa director said, "No. It's just the opposite. The worse people feel about themselves, the more they will invest on beauty treatments." The worse we feel about ourselves inside, the more time we will spend on the outside.

There is nothing wrong with the act of pampering oneself or having cosmetic surgery. Yet what *can* be dangerously wrong is why we do it. Any therapist, Christian or secular, will advise someone contemplating plastic surgery to resolve internal issues first.

Botox is a poison that eliminates wrinkles, but the botox philosophy may also be a poison for our souls. If we think that improving our looks will change our life or self-esteem, we will be sorely disappointed. As one woman pointed out, "I underwent a face-lift and received breast implants to become more attractive to men, only to find out that I attracted the wrong kind of men."

Did you know that God is the champion of improvement surgery? But superficial external procedures are not deep enough for God. He longs to perform radical surgery on us from the inside out, in the core of our souls. God performs open-heart surgery.

"A New You"

The ad in the upscale Los Angeles magazine promised "A New You" in six weeks, offering a variety of surgeries and a personal trainer. On the same page were ads for upscale matchmaking services. The blatant message was, "Become beautiful, then someone will love you."

The actual message is, "Become beautiful and someone will be attracted to you." Never confuse that with love. By definition, love is unconditional. Love is standing by someone when he or she looks his or her worst, is overweight or underweight, is at his or her wit's end, has a 103-degree fever, or is covered with a child's spit or vomit.

My friend Barb died on Mother's Day last year, leaving two teenage children and a grieving husband. She had a mastectomy in her early forties, but the cancer proceeded to ravage her body. Her husband adored her and said that she was the most beautiful woman he had ever known.

Another friend planned to donate one of her lungs to save her daughter who needed a lung transplant. Unfortunately her daughter died from cystic fibrosis two weeks before surgery. Yet another friend spent her midlife years nursing her invalid husband, wheelchair-bound, to his death.

Authentic love has nothing to do with having the perfect body or looking twenty years younger. It has everything to do with sacrifice.

Another ad promises increased self-confidence and esteem as a result of plastic surgery. Doctors claim that if you look better, you will feel better about yourself. Really? Actually the opposite is true. Genuine confidence and self-respect come from an acceptance and appreciation of oneself—faults and all—and evidences maturity. Family psychologist John Rosemond explains:

> *Our national obsession with attaining the supposed "cure-all" of high self-esteem (and making sure our children acquire it in abundance) has resulted in semantic confusion. People tend to think that self-confidence, self-respect and self-esteem are one and the same. . . . The difference between self-esteem and self-respect is not a mere matter of mincing words. The very real difference produces two entirely different sorts of people, and therefore two entirely different sorts of culture.*[1]

Feeling Invisible

We all have our stories about some of the "first times" in our midlife: The first time we were called ma'am. The first time we realized that men were staring at our teenage daughters, not even noticing us. The first time someone asked, "Were you pretty when you were young?" It *is* funny the first time it happens, but by the fiftieth time it's painful. First we feel unattractive, then invisible.

If we are athletes, dancers, musicians, or other professionals requiring physical agility, we are stunned to no longer have the energy, skills, or natural coordination that we took for granted twenty-five years ago. If we put our own pursuits on hold to raise children—thinking we would simply pick up where we left off—we are in for a rude awakening. We watch the Olympics and other exhibitions, fully aware that most competitors are twenty to thirty years younger than we are. Those in midlife are the parents and coaches of the competitors.

We need reading glasses to do the simplest tasks. If we don't write something down, we can't remember it. Women who have enjoyed perfect health all their adult life often begin to develop symptoms they have never experienced. It takes more time (and cosmetics) to make ourselves look "presentable" each morning. In a nutshell, we feel *less.*

Perhaps you already face physical challenges in your life. They will only become more dramatic during the midlife transition. I have thyroid disease and have always struggled with chemical depression and hormonal imbalances. I must regularly walk in the mornings to regulate the chemicals in my body. Midlife changes can feel like a roller coaster ride some days.

Like Mother, Like Daughter

> *Looking at the mother, you might hope that the daughter would become like her, which is a prospective advantage equal to a dowry—the mother too often standing behind the daughter like a malignant prophecy—"Such as I am, she will shortly be."*
>
> George Eliot, *Middlemarch*

The most serious issue arising today from commonplace plastic surgery is that younger and younger women (even teenage girls) are going under the knife. Family psychologists are concerned about the message young women are receiving. Breast enhancement surgery has become a popular high school graduation gift in some affluent circles.

We know that our physical appearance (and often personality) is a result of our genes. We resemble our parents, who resembled their parents, etc. We are part of a lineage, of people we dearly love. We also know that God does not make mistakes.

Many daughters look like their mothers. The old saying remains, "If you want to know what your girlfriend will look like in twenty-five years, just look at her mother." If we hate our bodies, our daughters will hate their bodies. If we resculpt our physical form, we communicate that we were ugly before surgery. Some of us reach back two generations. My mother is a vivacious woman with flair who loved to dance when she was young and always had a beautiful figure. At eighty-seven years of age, she can still dress to kill. Yet I am a carbon copy of my paternal grandmother, with opposite personality and physical traits of my own mother. Our genes are an undeniable part of who we are.

In a recent television interview, one middle-aged mother was trying to convince her beautiful sixteen-year-old daughter not to have liposuction and breast enhancement surgery. Yet the mother had undergone those two procedures a few months earlier. No matter what the mother said, her daughter was determined to fix her "ugly" body. Most daughters realize that they have younger versions of their mothers' physiques.

What messages are we communicating to our daughters? Has a less-than-perfect body become a deformed body? Children will always do what we do, rarely what we say. Talk truly is cheap. They will follow our example. What kind of model are we providing for our daughters, who will face their own midlife transitions?

Many midlife women try to look as young as their daughters. They want to be mistaken for an older sister, not a mother. As crazy as it sounds, some midlife women pursue relationships with younger men, sometimes even their daughters' boyfriends, desperately wanting to feel attractive and young again.

Some women want to relive their youth through their children, while others want to live a youth they personally never experienced. Each of us lives vicariously through our children to some extent, but as one wise woman told me, "I had my time. It's my daughter's turn now."

External vs. Eternal Goals

Is it unbiblical to have cosmetic surgery? Of course not. Is it unbiblical to wear braces or have a scar removed? Is it wrong to improve one's appearance? Of course not. While we model midlife confidence and acceptance for our daughters, we also want to model taking care of our physical health through exercise, a healthy diet, and preventive medicine.

The act of self-improvement itself is rarely unbiblical; the motives behind the act are what matter to God. He is much more concerned with the state of our mind and heart, our "interior," than our exterior. The questions are: What takes priority in our lives? What do we worship? Who do we trust? A simple test for what we worship in life is where we spend our two main resources—our time and money. God does not want us to focus on external goals but on eternal goals. So when you are experiencing any midlife blues about aging, remember to omit the X in your life: EXTERNAL vs. ETERNAL.

Have you ever encountered a person who seemed less than attractive until she or he began to talk, laugh, smile, and explode with the love of Jesus Christ? Before your eyes, this person transforms into an extraordinarily beautiful human being, attractive in the true sense of attracting others. You have also probably encountered someone who looked like a model until he or she became angry and said a cruel thing or spewed profanity. Beauty can transform into ugliness in just a few seconds.

We should be less concerned about changing our bodies and more concerned with changing our own eyes and how we view others. Do we judge others based on their physical appearance, their externals? The transformation needed in our culture can start with us.

Have you ever been pouring out your heart to a friend when, in the midst of the conversation, she grabbed her brush or lipstick to touch up her appearance? You immediately realized that throughout the entire discussion, she was distracted with thinking about her looks instead of listening to you. In big and small ways we communicate to people what we value. And on a grander scale, perhaps we become distracted with looking younger and more attractive and invest in that process more than in the needs of people around us.

Self-absorption is never attractive. People who focus on

others more than themselves can be absolutely mesmerizing, and it involves a transformation that cannot be achieved by a plastic surgeon.

Guidance from God's Word

If you have thought that the Bible does not speak specifically to our midlife issues, you will be surprised and encouraged to read God's words of guidance about our physical appearance and other midlife challenges.

Charm is a delusion and beauty fleeting;
it is the God-fearing woman who is honoured.

PROVERBS 31:30
THE NEW ENGLISH BIBLE

Your beauty should not come from outward adornment, such as braided hair and the wearing of gold jewelry and fine clothes. Instead, it should be that of your inner self, the unfading beauty of a gentle and quiet spirit, which is of great worth in God's sight. For this is the way that holy women of the past who put their hope in God used to make themselves beautiful.

1 PETER 3:3–5A

The life of the body is a tranquil heart,
but envy is a cancer in the bones.

PROVERBS 14:30

Beauty does not come from outward adornment or

comparing ourselves with others. True beauty comes from our inner selves, as we put our hope in God.

Questions for Journaling or Discussion

1. Do you focus on external or eternal goals when you view yourself? When you view others?

2. Do you struggle with judging others by their appearance? Do you use those judgments as a measuring stick for yourself?

3. By your actions, what messages do you communicate to your children? Though your children have left home, you remain their model, their compass.

4. On a piece of paper, label three categories:

    - Inner Beauty
    - Health
    - Outer Beauty

    List activities you spend time on in each category. Health (diet, exercise) can include activities that contribute to inner or outer beauty, depending on your motivation. Where do you spend the most time?

5. Describe the difference between love and attraction. Use examples from your own relationships.

God brings about birthdays . . . not as deadlines but lifelines. He builds them into our calendar once every year to enable us to make an annual appraisal, not only of our length of life but our depth. Not simply to tell us we're growing older . . . but to help us determine if we are also growing deeper.

Charles Swindoll

Children do not always listen to their parents, but they never fail to imitate them.

James Baldwin

Lord, remind me often that parents are intended to be a mooring post, a safe place to stay, a sure place to cast anchor come wind or weather.

Jill Briscoe

Midlife Glimpses

Susan thought that she had the perfect marriage and ideal family life. An article had actually appeared in the local newspaper, describing her picture-perfect family and their activities. Susan and her husband were committed Christians, active in their church, and homeschooled their seven children. Friends came to them for advice about their marriages. As a young boy, Susan's husband had watched his father, mother, and sister drown in a lake. He and his brother were raised by an abusive grandmother. Susan marveled at his ability to cope with that tragedy. Susan had also experienced an abusive childhood, and her husband had been her lifesaver, the steadfast rock in her life. Then in midlife, Susan's husband began experiencing severe depression and was diagnosed with an array of mental illnesses and was put on various medications. His erratic behavior and unpredictable emotions made Susan feel unsafe. After unsuccessfully seeking help from a variety of counselors, Susan's husband moved out. Susan returned to college with her older daughters, taking classes one night a week, with plans to complete a degree.

Jacquie believes that the two best gifts parents can give their children are a solid spiritual foundation and a debt-free education. When her children began leaving for college, she returned to her teaching career to pay for their tuitions at private Christian colleges. Two years before retirement, she was diagnosed with breast cancer. When her last child graduated from college, Jacquie celebrated her retirement and being a cancer survivor.

~

Tammy and her younger sister, Stacey, were legal guardians for one another's children in event of death. After Tammy's fourth and last child left home for college, Tammy and her husband were looking forward to traveling. Stacey and her husband were killed in a car accident just a few months later. Tammy and her husband are now raising Stacey's three children.

~

Lorraine married her college sweetheart and they had four children. After their last child left for college, Lorraine and her husband, both forty-nine, looked forward to enjoying their couple relationship. The day before their twenty-fifth wedding anniversary, Lorraine woke up to find her still husband beside her. With no warning, he had died from a massive heart attack during the night. Lorraine had suffered with bouts of depression throughout her life and she now felt that she was falling into a black hole. She experienced the classic stages of grief, from shock and depression to feeling angry that her husband had abandoned her in midlife. Lorraine was experiencing menopause and frequent headaches. In the midst of her own grief, she tried to comfort her young adult children, who were struggling with the loss of their father.

Slowly she began to build a new life. Lorraine had been a full-time mother and now applied for her first job in a local toy store. She enjoyed helping children and families. She started exercising. She rented an extra bedroom to students from a nearby college to ease the emptiness of living alone. She began a support group for other widows and widowers. Through this group, she met her second husband. They were married almost twenty years; the last ten years he suffered with Alzheimer's. Six months after his death, Lorraine's son died at age forty-seven from heart-related problems. Lorraine's grief was nearly unbearable. At age seventy-five, she enjoyed a whirlwind romance and married her third husband. She believes that each of her experiences with loss taught her important life lessons about appreciating loved ones. She views her life as three distinct chapters with the common thread of always feeling loved.

Chapter 4
Making Tough Choices

"Your life reminds me of an air traffic controller's job," my friend said to me.

If your life is like mine, for years you have coordinated countless take-offs and landings, often occurring simultaneously with various pilots traveling in different directions. You have kept your family members organized and safely on track, yet rarely have you personally taken the journey. The time has come for you to leave the tower.

When children leave home, our roles and purpose rapidly change. Whether we were 24/7 full-time mothers, or worked part time or full time while raising our families, our "job description" will never be the same. We are wrapping up one career, yet no one is throwing us a retirement party or giving us a congratulations bonus, not even a plaque honoring our years of service in motherhood. We are in one of the few careers where success means working oneself out of a job, with little acknowledgment (perhaps some type of closure ceremony *would* be helpful). We don't want to ever stop being supportive mothers, but we realize our roles need to change. Dorothy Canfield Fisher says it so well:

> *A mother is not a person to lean on but a person to make leaning unnecessary.*

As a wise friend told me, "Women can do anything well in life, just not all at the same time." We make choices along the way and then midlife arrives. Mothers that didn't work outside the home, enjoying motherhood as their primary career, wonder what will take its place. With skyrocketing college tuition costs, mothers who never intended to have second careers are forced to enter the job market to help with finances. Others are recruited into the work force because of a husband's job loss or an unexpected divorce.

Women who enjoyed exciting, fulfilling careers wonder if they spent enough time with their kids before they were gone. Women who worked full-time at less exciting jobs because of financial need, but would rather have been home with their children, wonder if they had the worst of all worlds.

Even midlife women who chose not to have families wonder if being childless for a lifetime was what they really wanted, and then it is often too late to reverse that decision.

The Crisis of Choices

In the middle of the journey of our life, I came to myself within a dark woods where the straight way was lost.

Dante Alighieri
The Divine Comedy

You have just read the most frequently quoted lines about midlife. Dante penned these words when he was forty-two years old. He had a wife and children. Dante had been fired from his job as one of the chief magistrates of Florence and was banished from the city because of his stand against the Pope. Dante was having a midlife meltdown. Then he wrote *The Divine Comedy*.

No one escapes honestly evaluating prior life choices. We each must make peace with the path we pursued before we can choose a future path. The operative word in a successful midlife journey is *choice*.

Why is the ability to make choices critical to surviving a potential crisis? Permit me to share with you a quick dose of Child Life/crisis counseling methodology, which not only influenced the way I parented but changed my approach to life as well. The Child Life department in a children's hospital is staffed with therapists who help pediatric patients cope with the crisis and trauma of hospitalization and illness.

The most important thing anyone can do for someone in crisis is to offer them choices. Simply knowing that we have choices, whether or not we act on them, diminishes our feelings of helplessness and powerlessness, which magnifies any emotional crisis.

For example, when working with hospitalized children, we as therapists cannot offer patients the option of having an IV treatment, but we *can* ask them in which arm they would prefer to have it given. We cannot give patients the option of leaving the hospital, but we *can* ask them what they want to eat for lunch. After lunch they had the choice of playing a game, painting a picture, or writing a song or poem.

The second most important thing we can do for someone facing a crisis is to help them prepare for it. The unknown is usually scarier than the known. For example, pediatric patients facing surgery can be educated about the procedure they will undergo. Child Life specialists explain the surgery and provide play therapy activities, where patients act out the procedure with dolls. Understanding leads to acceptance, diminishing fear.

How is this relevant for us? Remember, the best way to avoid a midlife meltdown is to prepare for it. The most difficult crisis is the one that takes us by complete surprise. We need time for "emotional play therapy" and role playing, to think through what the future holds and what options are available to us, hopefully before the day our child walks out the door.

If we feel that we have no choices about our future, we will feel angry, resentful, fearful, and helpless. If there is anything that midlife women have today, it is an abundance of choices. Being aware of our new opportunities is the most important step to making a successful midlife transition. The exploration of options is half the fun.

Abundant Options

Midlife mothers can start new careers, return to school, start new ministries, begin their own businesses, or immerse themselves in volunteer work—free from the daily demands of motherhood. Many women combine all those pursuits. Passions and interests that have been slowly developing through the years can merge into an incredible life adventure.

One of the advantages of our midlife stage is gaining perspective. We can see patterns in our lives, recognizing our natural bent. Understanding our God-given combination of talents and abilities, finely tuned with time and life experience, is the key to forging ahead in midlife.

I once believed that the best time to attend college was as a young person out of high school, when adult responsibilities were minimal (before house mortgages and families). Yet many people feel that young adulthood may be the worst time to attend college—a waste of time and money—unless the student is passionate about his or her field of interest. Too many college students remain in the exploratory stage for years, changing majors each semester, sometimes taking six or seven years to graduate. I know of several students who keep taking courses each semester in order to not lose their parents' health insurance benefits.

In contrast, midlife women who return to job training, college, or graduate school are exceptionally focused, insightful, excited about learning, and have vision and specific career goals.

They have no time to waste and are unusually productive. My good friend says, "School is a piece of cake after raising four children." Even women who have achieved successful first careers may be ready for a new challenge and want to enter different fields in their second careers.

Did you know that learning a new skill is also important to your physical health? Dendrites (your nerve cell extensions that communicate with other cells) increase with mental stimulation or decrease with a lack of stimulation. You cannot remain at the status quo. Your choices are to use it or lose it. Aerobic exercise increases blood flow and oxygen to the brain and is as important as mental exercise. Staying mentally and physically active is critical to midlife health.

Giving Back

The ability to show up brings with it the ability to grow up.
Julia Cameron

The psychologist Erik Erikson summed up healthy middle adulthood as the stage of generativity. We shift roles as we enter midlife, wanting to pass on our knowledge to younger people and give back to others what we received from our mentors. Erikson states that the alternatives are to become self-absorbed or stagnate.

I propose that empty nest parents face a double challenge. As parents, we have already transitioned to giving back to youth. We have been coaches for our children's sports teams, school volunteers, church youth leaders, youth music directors, band and athletic boosters, Girl Scout leaders, and more. Most of us have jumped at any opportunity to be involved in our children's lives and help other young people. Our ministries extended into the community. Midlife men and women are familiar with the stage of generativity.

Yet when our children begin leaving home, the opportunities wane. The door is no longer wide open. For example, it is no longer our turn to coach our son's soccer team or be the team mom. The parents of new team members want to be involved and should be. Many people remain involved with their children's prior activities, but in changing roles. They move into mentoring the mentors.

My husband and I were involved in leading musical productions in our church for twenty years. Our daughters both participated from their preschool years through high school, loving the world of music, dance, and dramatic performance. Music making was one of their connections with God and us.

Our younger son had no interest in choral music or staged musicals. He loved outdoor activities like baseball, rock climbing, and scuba diving. Therefore, my husband became involved in umpiring his Little League games and began training other umpires in our town. Realizing that church music was not going to be our son's path to a relationship with God, we needed to disciple our son a different way. As our daughters left home, we realized that the baton (literally) needed to be passed to other parents in our church, whose children remained musically involved.

These midlife transitions and role shifts are painful for empty nest parents. Not only are we missing our children, we miss the roles we played in their lives and in our community. We wonder if we have outlived our usefulness. We may feel "thrown away" in organizations and churches where we once were vitally involved.

Albert Einstein said, "Only a life lived for others is a life worthwhile." Passing along our skills and celebrating the success of the upcoming generation, instead of feeling threatened or replaced by them, requires tremendous maturity. Our transition to late adulthood depends on our shift in middle adulthood. Integrity in our later years comes from feeling that we lived responsible, caring lives, but despair sets in when we view our lives with regret.

Encouragement from God's Word

Commend what you do to Yahweh,
and your plans will find achievement.
PROVERBS 16:3

Yahweh will go in front of you,
and the God of Israel will be your rearguard.
ISAIAH 52:12B

My translation: God goes before you to plan the way; He comes behind you to hold you up.

Questions for Journaling and Discussion

1. Describe your changing roles through life:

   - before marriage
   - before children
   - while raising young children
   - while raising older children
   - while raising teens
   - today

   Have you ever had it all?

2. How have you given back to the next generation? Has that role changed as your children leave home?

3. Are you excited about the opportunity to start a new life adventure, or are you paralyzed with fear? You are probably somewhere in between. What options do you want to explore? Remember that God goes before you to plan the way and comes behind to hold you up (Isaiah 52:12b).

Assignment: Gather with a few close friends that are experiencing the empty nest to have a motherhood retirement party. Celebrate your years of service and remarkable achievement.

Life and faith always insist on moving forward; and I cannot move forward without leaving something behind.

Paul Tournier

God beckons us throughout life to have portable roots in order to advance in our earthly pilgrimage. Career crises remind us of our tentative status and present a challenge to continue our journey of faith.

Carnegie Samuel Calian

You cannot plan the future by the past.
Edmund Burke

Changes are not only possible and predictable, but to deny them is to be an accomplice to one's own necessary vegetation.
Gail Sheehy

Midlife Glimpses

Karen always enjoyed being a mother and especially liked working with young children. When her oldest daughter left for college, she began working toward a degree in early childhood education. When her younger daughter left the nest, Karen opened a preschool in her town. Karen finds it fulfilling to nurture other children as they grow and looks forward to being a grandmother someday.

Patty worked as a registered nurse until she stayed home to care for her children; one of her sons had learning disabilities. When her sons were older, she returned to school to complete a teaching credential. Since her sons became adults, she has been working in her local school district as a teacher. She especially enjoys teaching science and is committed to helping other children with learning problems while encouraging their parents.

With one daughter away at college, Lori entered a doctoral program in psychology. She originally had a degree in mathematics and chose to stay home to raise her two children. She and her husband divorced when their daughters were in high school. Through the years, she enjoyed working with children in the local schools and was a volunteer crisis counselor. She graduated from her Ph.D. program as her second daughter graduated from high school, and she began a post-doctoral internship at a nearby hospital.

Caroline had been too busy with her corporate career to pursue relationships. She married at age forty-eight. When she turned fifty she and her husband longed to share their love with someone else. With medical intervention, she became pregnant. She was ready for a new challenge in life. She took an early retirement from her company, continued part-time consulting, and enjoyed being home to raise her young son.

When her daughter left for college, Miriam was unprepared for how much she would miss her daughter. She was grateful for her continuing career that helped her get out of bed in the morning. Yet she questioned if she should have worked less and spent more time with her daughter when she was younger. Even when Miriam was with her daughter, she was exhausted at the end of each day. She regrets that she did not balance her career and motherhood in a more effective way.

Katharine Graham was the perfect supportive wife, raising four children. Her husband, Phil Graham, ran the Washington Post Company. He suffered with manic depression, hiding his secret from the world until he committed suicide. At age forty-six Katharine Graham became president of the Washington Post Company and six years later became its publisher. She courageously changed her life, the newspaper industry, and the history of our nation.

Karen Hughes, counselor to President Bush, made the agonizing decision to leave her full-time position at the White House mid-term. She moved with her family back to Texas (where she first worked for Governor Bush) to spend more time with her husband and son. Her teenage son had never adapted well to life in Washington and missed his friends and former life. Hughes, a devout Christian, was torn for months between the pressing responsibilities of her job and her role as mother and wife. Though the path has not been easy, she never regretted her decision to put her family first. She now consults with President Bush from her home office in Texas.

~

Victoria's hopes for attending college were never realized when her home life fell apart during her senior year in high school. Her father left his family for another woman and her mother became an alcoholic. There was neither money nor emotional support for Victoria to reach her goals. She also had reading difficulties, forcing her to work unusually hard in school. Her passions were art, science, and helping people, yet she wondered if she was capable of attending college. After graduating from high school, Victoria volunteered at a convalescent hospital, where she was inspired to pursue the occupational therapy field.

After taking some courses at a local junior college, Victoria left school to marry and have a family. She raised two children; her son had learning disabilities similar to her own. Through helping her son and working as a special education instructional aide, she remembered her dream to become a therapist. When Victoria's older daughter was accepted to college, she learned that if two family members were attending college simultaneously, more grant money was available. Her daughter's education would be less expensive if Victoria returned to college. Though not confident in her abilities, Victoria enrolled in a state university and completed her degree in social science. As a fifty-year-old grandmother, she entered a master's program in occupational therapy, surviving twelve-hour days, a long commute to another city, and rigorous internship training. When Victoria's mom required home hospice care, Victoria spent the weekends caring for her mother in addition to her school demands.

Victoria's husband, Mike, was her greatest cheerleader, supporting her in every way to reach her dream. They took out loans for her education and Mike took on all the household chores. He told friends, "Victoria gave up her dream to marry me and it's my turn to give that back to her." Sacrifices were required of both of them. Today Victoria is head of the occupational therapy department for a large school district and enjoys consulting with teachers, working with children and families, and giving seminars. She wants every midlife woman to know that it is never too late to realize one's dreams. Victoria is not only an inspiration to other women but also an exceptional role model for her granddaughters.

Chapter 5
The "In-Between" Generation

She is clothed in strength and dignity,
She can laugh at the days to come.
Proverbs 31:25

If you are nearing fifty years of age, as I am, you were raised in a unique era of women's roles. We are the "in-between" generation. We reaped the educational and professional benefits that the feminists of the 1960s fought for. We enjoyed abundant opportunities offered to women in the university setting and workplace. We did not become 1950s homemakers, but they were the women who nurtured and influenced us.

Our mothers were happy to see us succeed professionally and have opportunities they didn't, but they still expected us to marry, raise a family, and maintain perfect homes as they did. As long as we added the "MRS. degree" to our other accomplishments, they were content. Hence the "superwoman" approach was born. Women of our generation were expected to do it all. No wonder the divorce rate skyrocketed. Wives were working one shift in the workplace and a second shift at home, while their husbands continued to only work one shift in the workplace. These men were also raised and influenced by 1950s homemakers. Then the feminist pendulum swung too far and, with our new opportunities, we lost former privileges.

I laugh when my mother and mother-in-law share their worries about my twenty-two-year-old daughter not having any marriage prospects. I try to explain to them that the world has radically changed. Young women today want to experience life, travel, and establish fulfilling careers. When they do find a life partner, they will marry for love and friendship, not because they feel pressured or desperate. Our daughters are marrying men who are true partners, willing to share all of life's responsibilities.

Today's generation of young women does not dream of marrying a doctor, lawyer, minister, or other professional as their grandmothers did. They are confidently applying to law school, medical school, seminary, and other graduate programs, rather than planning weddings as they graduate from college. Our wedding occurred the day after I graduated from college, and my husband had finished graduate school (both of our parents felt strongly that we should not marry before we completed our educations). I applied to graduate school while planning a wedding, a perfect example of the "in-between" generation. I remember my supportive mom feeling a little baffled about why I was pursuing graduate education if I was married.

Neither have those of us nearing fifty been part of a fighting generation. We did not have to fight for women's rights. Those pioneers went before us. Similarly, we did not have to fight feminists when we decided to stay home to raise our children. A *Wall Street Journal* article in 1993 stated that the stay-at-home mom was fast becoming the newest status symbol of the conscientious 1990s.

Fifty years after Simone de Beauvoir and Betty Friedan described full-time mothers and homemakers as mindless parasites who would only find their value in the workplace, the majority of society has acknowledged that child-care workers can be paid to feed, bathe, and care for young children but they can never be paid to love them. "Children need more than food, shelter, and clothing. They need at least one person who is crazy about them," said Fran Stott. Ideally one parent, whether mother or father (or both with creative scheduling) can provide children with around-the-clock care by someone who is crazy about them. Sometimes a loving relative can also help.

Simone de Beauvoir stated in 1975, "No woman should be authorized to stay at home to raise her children." Ironically, the same early feminists who were championing women's rights were bent on robbing them of their choices. In Soviet bloc countries, women were forced to enter the workplace, leaving their young children in institutional child-care facilities. When these countries were freed from communism, women rejoiced in the choice to remain at home to raise their families.

Our generation has had the best of all worlds, the privilege to choose different paths during each season of life. Our individual choices have been respected by our peers and society. We paved the way for our daughters. Yet our "in-between" generation faces unusual challenges when entering midlife. Perhaps we lack a pioneer spirit in forging a new path.

Can Anyone Have it All?

Rosanna Arquette was inspired to film the movie *Searching for Debra Winger* by another movie she viewed as a child, *The Red Shoes.* In *The Red Shoes,* a dancer must choose between her ballet career and getting married and having a family. She cannot make the decision, so she throws herself in front of a train, committing suicide. Arquette talks to many midlife actresses about the choices they have made, wrestling with the questions, "Can women have it all? How do we choose? And how do we face midlife in light of those choices?" Debra Winger, who chose in her midlife years to leave the movie industry to raise a family, shares, "Anyone who says you don't have to make sacrifices to raise children is lying."

Some of my favorite female music professors, who were world-class concertizing performers, had chosen not to marry or have children. They often had live-in personal assistants, allowing them to wholeheartedly pursue their careers. Through the years, I've sometimes wondered what I could accomplish if I had a wife (another name for a personal assistant), someone who would change the sheets, clean the house, go to the market, transport my children, have dinner on the table, pay the bills, buy birthday gifts for relatives, and do all the other tasks that fill my days. A product of the "in-between" generation, I've tried to pursue a part-time career while being a personal assistant to each of my family members. I am committed to their success.

Myth of the Bookmark Effect

"Do you ever regret your decision to stay home with your kids? Was the sacrifice too great? Do you ever feel that your background was completely wasted?" A close friend asked me these questions one day. I could have given her a great speech about how motherhood draws on every bit of one's training and expertise (which I do believe). Instead I honestly responded, "Don't ask me that on a bad day."

The truth is that I never viewed motherhood as a sacrifice because I enjoyed it so much. At times, the privilege of being with my kids as much as I desired felt quite selfish.

When we are young mothers, we do not purposefully plan to put our lives on hold for twenty-five years. But as our families grow and the demands multiply, we naturally give up more of our own agenda. Sometimes we don't even remember what our agenda was. We live with the vague idea that when our children leave home, we can pick up where we left off—the bookmark effect. We view our lives as happily interrupted, not derailed.

But once we hit midlife we realize that our lives are not books, where we can open to the chapter we were in the middle of (before motherhood) and keep going. We cannot pick up an established career after a twenty-year hiatus and expect to re-enter at the same level. We cannot return as a student to a university that we attended twenty-five years ago and expect things to be the same. We certainly cannot expect to be competitive with our peers who have been working for the past thirty years without a break or with new graduates who are current on the latest research.

We have to start over. The opportunities a brand-new start can offer are incredibly exciting for some women and paralyzing for others. Many women enter fields they never even contemplated when they were in their twenties. They are different people today because of thirty years of wisdom and experience. While Sheehy called this opportunity the "bonus stage," Margaret Mead labeled this renewed energy in midlife females as "postmenopausal zest." Anne Morrow Lindbergh wrote:

> *Purposeful giving is not as apt to deplete one's resources; it belongs to that natural order of giving that seems to renew itself even in the act of depletion. The more one gives, the more one has to give—like milk in the breast.*[1]

The key to the midlife career transition is to continue giving. To be proactive, not reactive. Many of our most beloved novels, musical works, and artistic creations were produced by midlife artists. We enjoy a different perspective when we reach our middle years.

Acceptance vs. Resignation

While dining together, I shared with a close friend that I had come to terms with the choices I had made in life and accepted the path I was on. I was feeling quite spiritual about making peace with God's will in my midlife years. Her answer jolted me. "What I hear from you is not acceptance. It is resignation, and that is not biblical. That is not what God calls us to do. God guides moving vessels." Wouldn't I have given my children the same speech? I thought long and hard about that revelation.

Resignation is giving up. Do we follow a God of resignation or a God who moves mountains, parts the Red Sea, and leads people on the most unexpected, surprising journeys? The last thing the Creator of the Universe, who can do anything, wants in His followers is a spirit of resignation. He wants us to have a spirit of expectancy.

Throughout my years, God had consistently turned my life upside down with outrageous surprises, twists, and turns. I could list miracle after miracle. Did I think that the miracles had stopped because I was a midlife female? I didn't expect much and was living as if my best, most productive years were behind me. I felt like I didn't belong anywhere. I was entering that dark midlife tunnel, described to me by many women, no longer fitting into my old life but unable to grasp an intangible new life.

I felt that I was permanently stuck in God's waiting room. Waiting for what? . . . I couldn't imagine. One of my favorite quotes, which I was so quick to share with others who worried about the future, had always been: *God only gives us the ticket when we get to the train station* (Corrie ten Boom).

But I was feeling like I had already been at the train station for a while, and there was no visible ticket. I had lost my confidence, though intellectually I knew that my confidence should only rest in God. The truth is that I had forgotten how to take risks, like the trapeze artist who must let go of one bar before reaching for the next one. I had forgotten how to let go, trusting that God would catch me.

Encouragement from God's Word

A man's heart plans out his way
But it is Yahweh who makes his steps secure.
PROVERBS 16:9

Hard work always yields its profit,
Idle talk brings only want.
PROVERBS 14:23

Questions for Journaling or Discussion

1. Are you part of the "in-between" generation? Did you try to do it all? What was your mother's influence on you? How does she influence you today? How did your husband's mother influence him?

2. Have you experienced the myth of the bookmark effect?

3. Imagine that you are lost and alone, driving down a dark, treacherous mountain road. Then a friend drives by, motioning you to follow her. It is one thing to say that you trust your friend; it is another to actually follow her down the mountain. Only when we are feeling lost do we actually follow. If you are feeling adrift or lost during your midlife transition, view this as a remarkable opportunity to completely trust and follow God. Which of your close friends would you trust to lead you down the mountain? Why would you trust God any less?

Somewhere along the line of development we discover what we really are, and then we make our real decision for which we are responsible. Make that decision primarily for yourself because you can never really live anyone else's life, not even your own child's. The influence you exert is through your own life and what you become yourself.

Eleanor Roosevelt

You can be too big for God to use, but you cannot be too small.

Nelle Reagan

Midlife Glimpses

I've always believed that one woman's success can only help another woman's success.

Gloria Vanderbilt

In their late thirties:

Alice M. Birney founded a parent organization that became the PTA.

Mother Teresa founded the Missionaries of Charity Sisterhood.

Janet Guthrie was the first woman to drive in the Indianapolis 500.

In their forties:

Joan G. Conney introduced *Sesame Street* to television.

Harriet Beecher Stowe published *Uncle Tom's Cabin.*

Margaret Rudkin started a business baking bread for her neighbors. She named it after her farm in Connecticut, *Pepperidge Farm.*

Ruth Handler and her husband created the Barbie doll.

Rosa Parks refused to give up her seat on a bus in Birmingham, Alabama.

Maria Montessori opened her first Montessori school in New York.

Marie Curie won the Nobel Prize in chemistry. She was the first person to win two Nobel Prizes.

Anna Taylor was the first person to make it over the Niagara Falls alive in a barrel.

Julia Child wrote the bestselling cookbook *Mastering the Art of French Cooking.*

Estée Lauder introduced her first successful skin care product. She had always made creams in her kitchen, inspired by her uncle who was a chemist. Called one of the world's greatest entrepreneurs, she built a $5 billion business.

~

In their fifties:

Beverly Sills became the director of the New York City Opera.

Dian Fossey published *Gorillas in the Mist,* her study of apes in the African rain forest.

Sandra Day O'Connor became the first woman to serve on the U.S. Supreme Court.

Juliette Gordon Low founded the first troop of Girl Guides in America, which became the Girl Scouts.

Under the pen name George Eliot, Mary Ann Evans published *Middlemarch.*

Margaret Thatcher was the first woman to be elected prime minister of Britain.

Jan Karon left a successful business career to write the bestselling *Mitford* series.

Toni Morrison wrote her most well-known book, *Beloved.*

Clara Barton founded the American Red Cross.

Madeleine Albright was the first woman named U.S. Secretary of State.

Chapter 6
Treasure in Our Own Backyards

Your diamonds are not in far distant mountains or yonder seas; they are in your own backyard, if you but dig for them.

—Russell H. Conwell

In midlife, most women realize that our lives have rarely turned out as we had planned or imagined them. Most of us appreciate that the detours were better than our original plan. Other women wish they could turn the clock back and start over again.

In a way, this book you are reading is a sequel (twenty years and ten books later) to *What's a Smart Woman Like You Doing in a Place Like This,* which was the product of my first life transition meltdown. My first book was the ramblings of a sleep-deprived twenty-five-year-old new mother who was trying to sort out her changing life. I have come full circle. The book you are now holding is the ramblings of a forty-nine-year-old mother, in transition again, still trying to sort out her changing life and still sleep deprived, not because of a nursing infant, but because of teenagers coming home at curfew or overseas phone calls from our daughter who is studying abroad.

In the midst of the ramblings, the premise of *What's a Smart Woman...?* remains valid today. Every woman is a specialized professional and entrepreneur, regardless of monetary compensation. Understanding the true definition of these words is the key:

Professional: defined as one engaged in a calling requiring specialized knowledge and preparation; a principal calling, vocation, or employment.

Career: defined as a profession undertaken as a permanent calling with progressive achievement.

Entrepreneur: defined as one who organizes, manages, and assumes the risks of an enterprise (purposeful project).

Whether we are new mothers or midlife mothers, or weaving career pursuits into our lives, involved in volunteer work or church ministries, we remain professionals and entrepreneurs, no matter if we receive a salary or have an impressive title.

I had assumed that I would return to work after my maternity leave twenty-four years ago. But like many women, after holding my firstborn daughter, I knew that I would never leave her by choice. I did wonder if I would regret the hiatus someday, but I can honestly say today that I don't have any regrets over the time I chose to spend with each of my children, being completely available to them. This experience of motherhood has been my greatest privilege, and I am grateful that our financial situation allowed me the choice.

Yet my encounter with Lisa (from chapter two) challenged me to brainstorm about ways that I could continue working in my field without being separated from my children. How could I not "give up everything for them," as Lisa angrily perceived motherhood, and perhaps even enhance my children's lives with creative pursuits? The result was that I started my own business. I am indebted to Lisa, who helped avert a future midlife meltdown for me. I want other young mothers to know that the best time to plan for a midlife transition is years before you reach it.

Buried Treasure

The main reason I started my own business was that I didn't want to have a twenty-five-year gap in my resume when I went on a midlife job search and then blame my family for it. I was also keenly aware of the need to be a productive role model for my daughters. Just as I had assumed that I would return to work six months after my daughter's birth, I assumed that I would reenter the full-time work force at midlife.

My home business started out with teaching music to my own children and their friends and writing articles for professional journals. I believed that if I could not communicate the joy of music to my own children, I had no business teaching other parents' children.

As my children grew, my business grew. I added group classes to my curriculum and began specializing in teaching music to children with special needs, my original career choice. I began publishing music arrangements. As a volunteer, I helped with music programs in my children's schools. My husband and I led the church music ministry. My children were fully involved in this developing music community and enjoyed it as much as we did.

I never intended to become a professional author. That thought simply didn't cross my mind. I began writing when my daughter was an infant because I didn't have anyone to talk with and needed a way to communicate. It's amazing how some of our best experiences in life are the surprises that we never could have planned or envisioned. I continued writing articles and they lengthened into books. I contacted a well-known writer one day about two crazy book ideas. She offered to become my agent and sold them both within two weeks, bid on by two different publishers. I was too young and naïve to realize how rare that was.

Through the years, I continued to work on book projects, helped with a young writers' group for my daughter's class, and participated in a women's journal writers' group.

When I left the work force twenty-five years ago, I was a creative-arts therapist in a children's hospital completing doctoral research, supervising interns, teaching music therapy at the university level, and performing often as a musician. Before becoming pregnant, I envisioned a solid career path, longing to make significant contributions to helping children. All that came to a screeching halt when we moved across the state for my husband's job promotion. I had an emotional meltdown when I was removed from every activity I loved as well as friends and family. Then I became pregnant, with "morning sickness" that lasted all day for months. My peers were convinced that I had committed professional suicide.

In hindsight, I did commit professional suicide. I have never regretted staying home with my children, but I did regret having to choose between the two lives.

I also took a hard line, making a conscious decision to pursue an endeavor only if it benefited my own children and did not take me away from them. If I was going to be home with my kids, then I was literally going to be home and completely available to my family. When my children were older, I taught music during the day while they were at school. The criteria I had was simple—simple in theory, not so simple in practice. As I turned down book signings, professional workshops, speaking engagements, radio interviews, and other opportunities, my stand became unpopular. I tried to explain to my publisher of *What's a Smart Woman...*, "Why would I write a book about leaving the workforce to stay home with one's children and then leave my own children to go talk about it?"

My stand hasn't changed through the years, no matter the ages of my children, and remains equally unpopular. I arrived at midlife, not regretting for one minute the path I had chosen, but sometimes wishing that I could have taken both paths. Then I realized that God *had* taken me down both paths, but in ways I didn't recognize. It was almost as if He hit me on the side of the head.

I was unable to pursue working with hospitalized children,

but I certainly had worked with many children in similar need. I was unable to pursue teaching at the college level, but I had continued researching and writing books that were used as textbooks in university classes. With every dream that I thought I had sacrificed, I realized that God had fulfilled it in a radically different way. He had merged my passions and desires with His purposes.

When I struggled with finding time to write in the midst of my family demands, I remembered Katherine Paterson's words:

> *. . . success might have come sooner if I'd had a room of my own and fewer children, but I doubt it. For as I look at my writing, it seems to me that the very persons who took away my time and space are the ones who have given me something to say.*[1]

My family members *were* the ones who gave me something to say. Only in midlife could I identify that journey. My business had developed into a solid career, better than any job I would find working for someone else. I had found treasure buried in my own backyard, yet I did not completely dig it up and dust it off until midlife.

What treasure has been buried in your own backyard? If you are like other midlife women, you have been honing your skills and cultivating a midlife path for years. You just haven't stepped back to identify it yet. You haven't had the time to recognize what God has already done.

Guidance from God's Word

True Buried Treasure

Yes, if your plea is for clear perception,
if you cry out for discernment,
if you look for it as if it were silver,
and search for it as for buried treasure,
you will then understand what the fear of Yahweh is,
and discover the knowledge of God.
For Yahweh himself is giver of wisdom,
from his mouth issue knowledge and discernment.
He keeps his help for honest men,
he is the shield of those whose ways are honorable;
he stands guard over the paths of justice,
he keeps watch on the way of his devoted ones.

PROVERBS 2:3–8

Do not store up for yourselves treasures on earth, where moth and rust destroy, and where thieves break in and steal. But store up for yourselves treasures in heaven, where moth and rust do not destroy, and where thieves do not break in and steal. For where your treasure is, there your heart will be also.

MATTHEW 6:19–21

Questions
for Journaling or Discussion

1. What is the treasure buried in your own backyard? What are your skills, abilities, and experiences that have prepared you for this bonus stage of life?

2. Did God provide a way to accomplish your original life goals and dreams in a different way?

3. How has your family given you something to say, an unexpected expertise?

4. When we are devoted to God, He keeps watch on our way. Read Proverbs 2:38 and describe the true buried treasure we should be seeking.

5. What does Matthew 6:21 reveal in your life? What treasures are you storing up? Where is your heart?

My writing is a way to harness my creative energy, while mentally flossing my brain. . . . Mothering children has added more depth to my writing. My published articles are a testament that having children is not the end of creativity, but the beginning.

Mary Kenyon

When I went through those experiences I thought them privations and losses; now I saw them treasure chests of insight. What countless riches lay buried under the ground of those early years that I had thought so black, so barren. . . .

Anzia Yezierska
Bread Givers

I have been happy in every period of my adult life: attending college and law school, practicing law, staying at home to raise a family, and creating a new life once my family responsibilities had largely ended. Yet those many years I spent as a mother at home from the birth of my first child until the last left for college were the best, the ones I would be least willing to have forgone. Feminists recount endless tales of women's oppression throughout the ages, but one of the greatest injustices to women is feminists' own success in convincing society to treat as a sacrifice what for some women can be the most rewarding occupation of their lives.

F. Carolyn Graglia

Domestic Tranquility: A Brief Against Feminism[2]

Midlife Glimpses

Nancy, an amateur photographer, was a publicist/historian for her children's school events. After her children graduated, the local newspaper offered her a job as a photojournalist.

Marie always enjoyed cooking for her large family and friends. When her children left home, she became involved with a church food bank. She now regularly organizes and cooks meals for the homeless in her town.

Free of her children's busy schedules, Jennifer became head of the women's ministries program in her large church. She organizes weekly Bible studies, discipleship groups, monthly luncheons, and annual retreats. She coordinates special speakers for the events and, to her surprise, has enjoyed being a speaker herself.

Diane was a full-time mom who usually ended up organizing events and being in positions of leadership for a variety of her children's activities. When her children left home, she returned to school to pursue a business degree and now holds a corporate position.

Kris had worked as a registered nurse before having children. She continued to help elderly people in the church on a volunteer basis. When her children left home, she began working as a home care nurse. Soon her husband's parents required similar care, yet they were not comfortable with strangers. Kris offered her services to care for her in-laws and they gratefully accepted.

~

Tania was passionate about theater and dance in college. Yet nightly rehearsals and weekend performances did not mix with raising a family of four children. She put her love of performing on hold but continued to help with her children's school and church productions. After her children left for college, Tania became involved with her local community theater and began auditioning for different productions in neighboring cities.

~

Susan had always enjoyed quilting. After her children left home, she became a volunteer at a local hospital. She noticed a need and knew she could help. She began making quilts, intended to wrap stillborn babies in for burial, as gifts for grieving families.

~

Donna had majored in Christian education at Biola College before marrying and staying home to raise her three sons. She homeschooled her children and remained active in organizing discipleship programs in the churches she attended. She worked as a receptionist at her eldest son's high school to be near him during his senior year. As her children prepared to leave home, her passion for writing sustained her. She joined a writers' critique group, wrote a book and a Bible study series, and penned a play for her son's high school drama department. With the encouragement of her writers' group, Donna adapted her play into a screenplay, which placed as a quarterfinalist in two major competitions. She is currently working on her second book and pursuing opportunities for her screenplay to be made into a film. Donna and her husband remain active in lay ministry, mentoring other believers.

~

When fifty-nine-year-old Edie Munger set out to pursue a Ph.D. in clinical psychology, she was told by a professor that she was too old to achieve her goal. Four years later she was the first woman to graduate from Fuller Seminary's School of Psychology and was later named director of the Creative Counseling Center at Hollywood Presbyterian Church. She had left her career as a clinical social worker to further her education, and many people felt that her goals were too lofty for a pastor's wife.

Nanci, a doctor's wife and mother of three sons, had always enjoyed sharing the dramatic arts with children. When her sons began leaving home, she started volunteering at a children's hospital, using puppets and creative drama activities to help patients. She entered a masters' degree program in creative dramatics at a nearby university, researching the effects of puppet therapy on pediatric patients.

Chapter 7
Facing Your Spouse's Midlife Challenges

But those who marry will face many troubles in this life, and I want to spare you this.
—1 Corinthians 7:28b

Taken out of context, this biblical verse is comical. Some scholars believe that Paul was married because to have held his leadership position before conversion would have required marriage. Perhaps his wife died; we do not know. Paul advised his Christian brothers and sisters to remain as they were because of the challenging times they lived in. If they were married, they should remain married. If single, they should remain single. The relevant message for us is that when a crisis comes, marriage is often the more complicated, harder road. Most married people would attest to that fact. Ideally a lifelong companion should make life more tolerable, but often that is not reality.

I met my husband when I was a seventeen-year-old freshman in college. He was two years older. I had just become a Christian and was attending a Bible study he was leading. I wrote to my parents about the young man who was discipling me. My mom laughed, saying that was the funniest dating tactic she had ever heard about.

John was a biochemistry major, but his passion was music.

John's biochemistry professor said he would agree to be John's thesis advisor in exchange for a favor. The professor's wife wanted to start a youth choir at their church and needed a director. John agreed to be the youth choir director and asked me to be the accompanist. Since that day we have worked together in different churches with a variety of choirs for thirty years.

John was the brightest, most exciting young man I had ever met. He was my complete opposite in every way—lively, fun, spontaneous, and risk taking. He made me laugh, loved to bend the rules, lived life on the edge, and never bored me. He was everything I wasn't but wanted to be. The first present he ever bought me was a pair of hiking boots for mountain explorations. He taught me to drive his fast car with a 5-speed stick. Life was one thrilling adventure after another with him. As our relationship matured, I became his anchor, the safe, stable retreat from the chaos of his world. We were as different as could be.

John and I met in a way that is considered old-fashioned today—before the advent of online chat rooms, upscale dating services, and compatibility screening. No sane person would have matched us based on our compatibility.

Do opposites attract and then drive each other crazy for a lifetime? My children say that opposites complement and balance each other. I say it's a little of both and requires unflinching commitment. Constant adventures are fun . . . but exhausting on a regular basis. Whether you are in an ideally compatible marriage or married your opposite like I did, be prepared for some of your toughest marriage challenges to occur in midlife.

Male Menopause

More midlife literature has been written about the male midlife crisis (sometimes called male menopause) than any other topic. Similar to female hormones, men's hormones change with decreasing levels of testosterone being secreted into the bloodstream, which can cause depression. I thought the male midlife crisis was a joking matter until some of my friends' husbands (men who I considered perfect, godly husbands and fathers) began leaving their families. And as I learned from Lisa, there are also wives and mothers who, after taking care of everyone else's needs for decades, decide to take care of themselves after their kids leave home, and file for divorce.

One of the most significant factors affecting your adjustment to midlife will be how your husband manages his midlife transition. We are foolish to think that Christian couples are immune to this challenge, just as Christian teens are not immune to pregnancy, drugs, and alcohol. Preparation, hard work, and being aware of midlife pitfalls is critical. Authentic faith and trusting in God are our anchors. An ounce of prevention is truly worth a pound of cure.

Change

In working with terminally ill children, I was surprised to learn that the divorce rate for grieving parents is high. I incorrectly assumed that two people who experienced the illness and death of their child would share a deep bond for life. The truth is that two drowning people cannot save each other. Coping with loss of any kind is stressful for couples, because we grieve and adjust to change in varied ways.

Does the word "change" have positive or negative connotations for you? Change has rarely been a positive experience for me. In my mind, change translates into losing something I love. Relocating is difficult. Losing people I care for is painful. Adjustment comes slowly for me. In contrast, my husband loves the word "change." He lives for change and new adventures.

I grew up in the same house from kindergarten through

high school. Stability and safety are comforting to me. I cherish my friends whom I have known since I was five years old. My husband's family moved around the country due to his father's position as an aeronautical engineer with NASA. While the unknown is terrifying to me, the unknown is exciting for John. He enjoys pursuing new experiences, especially traveling to remote, exotic locations.

The way you and your husband each approach multiple changes in life will define your midlife transition and, later, your retirement years. Your families are changing, your bodies are changing, your jobs are changing, and more. One of you may be grieving the losses while the other is anticipating the coming opportunities. Hopefully your approaches will balance each other, but often conflicts are inevitable as coping methods collide. Be sensitive to how you each process change. In the midst of all the changes in your midlife marriage, it is good for you and your spouse to remind each other of how our God does not change.

Common Pitfalls

> *When asked why he decided to write a novel at age fifty, Umberto Eco replied: "Some men at that age take up with chorus girls. I wrote a novel instead."*

There is no better time to work on your marriage than when you face the empty nest. If you have been on autopilot during these past busy, stressful years, it's time to take back the controls, which requires tremendous effort. Many people have unknowingly used their kids and careers as buffers against a deteriorating relationship. We argue about the kids, schedules, money, our parents, and more, thinking, "Well, at least if we are arguing, we are communicating." But as we have decreasing topics to argue about, we may also have less to talk about.

Women who have emotionally invested in relationships

with their children to combat the inattention and neglect of busy husbands, find themselves especially vulnerable when the children leave home.

Becoming aware of common conflicts between partners can help prepare us for midlife marriage. Thinking about the following pitfalls and discussing them before they take us by surprise may help us avoid a marriage meltdown.

Pitfall #1—The Flip-Flop

The classic conflict between midlife couples occurs when the wife is ready for a new career or adventure while the husband's career is winding down and he is preparing for retirement. Forced early retirement due to downsizing is especially painful. Late middle-age men are most at risk for job termination, and finding a new job is difficult.

The wife, after raising the children, has been waiting for "her time." She is blossoming, exploring new opportunities, while her husband is now waiting for her. She may be working or attending night classes instead of at home preparing meals for a hungry family. The same man who had little time to nurture his wife when their children were young and he was building his career twenty years ago is now ready for more relationship time. He still wants to eat dinner together when he comes home from work. Their roles have reversed, and the wife is torn. She doesn't want her lonely husband to find a relationship elsewhere, nor does she want to stop pursuing her new dreams and goals.

Pitfall #2—The Myth of the Greener Grass

Temptation is everywhere. Those of us in the baby boomer generation face added challenges. Viagra is available. The Internet has made emotional affairs easy with chat rooms and pornography. Developing addictions is all too common in midlife as people use alcohol or other "medications" to numb pain, depression, and despair.

Phenylethylamine (PEA) is a natural substance in the brain that gives us a chemical high. We can experience PEA by participating in high-risk sports or through infatuations and attractions (which I consider equally dangerous sports). Engaging in high-risk sports and affairs (sexual or emotional) offers a similar "rush" and is common in midlife. The truth is that being in the company of younger, attractive women *does* make midlife men feel young again. The loss of youth is a legitimate loss.

Discuss as a couple your strategies to be on guard against temptation. Similar to what we tell our teenagers, don't put yourself in a potentially unsafe situation. Even though midlife is typically anything but boring, it can feel boring at times. We get hungry for a little excitement. Obedience to God leads to peace, but not to a chemical rush. Understand the critical difference between God's peace and boredom.

Midlife experts agree that one of the red flags of a serious midlife crisis is when one's behavior is completely out of character. As one wife described it, "My husband had always been rock solid. Yet when he was nearing fifty, he began having coffee outside the office with a younger female co-worker, and he decided to try skydiving. This was a man I didn't know anymore."

Pitfall #3—Managing the Money

Midlife couples paying high college tuitions for their children already feel financially strapped, but suddenly the husband wants to buy a sports car, boat, or other "boy toy" or invest financially in a dream that has been on hold. Many wives have told me about their husband's extravagant purchases while adding, "I guess it's better than having an affair." Financial disputes are rarely about money; they are about power and who has control over the money, especially when difficult choices must be made.

Negotiating Midlife Dreams

As an elementary school student, my husband spent many hours standing outside in the hall as punishment. He had to peer through the classroom window as his teacher taught because he could not sit still or stop talking. John is just as active today.

As a young person, my husband made a conscious choice that he would live life to the fullest, because one never knew when one's life would end. Because his father died in midlife, John was not about to wait until midlife or retirement to engage in activities he loved. He has immersed himself in numerous sports and hobbies through the years. In the beginning of our relationship, before having children, I tried to participate in his passions. Yet I couldn't figure out how to get off the chairlift while learning to ski. I broke my tailbone while in-line skating, I became terribly seasick while racing sailboats, I spent more time untangling my fishing line from the bushes than in the stream. I was willing to try everything, but ended up being more of a hindrance than a help. As our children grew, they became involved in John's activities and loved the excitement.

When John started scuba diving, I never even entertained the thought of trying that sport because my failure to succeed could be life-threatening. I assumed John would immerse himself in this new sport and be on to another one in a couple of years. But soon our children became capable divers, traveling with their dad on dive boats (our oldest daughter even works on a dive boat during the summer season).

And then to my surprise, my husband decided that scuba diving would be his midlife career. I never expected to hear my fun-loving, positive husband say that he felt trapped in his corporate job and was feeling depressed. This was new territory for us. Ten years earlier, John had left a job to start his own business, which was quite successful. He bought a Mustang convertible a few years later, and I thought that we had averted a full-blown midlife crisis. Yet John was now preparing for his "midlife event." In addition to his corporate day job, he pursued extensive training to become a scuba diving instructor. Then as a trainer of other instructors, he began traveling to remote dive sites around the world and bought a scuba diving shop. Diving had suddenly become our lives.

I had always tried to support John's dreams and passions, realizing that this zest for life was intertwined with the very core of his being. Yet this unexpected midlife shift in our lives was a real stretch for me.

I believe that a spouse should be his or her partner's best cheerleader, encouraging them in all their endeavors, never squashing their dreams. Isn't this how we raise our children? Our spouses deserve no less. This is one of the most important ways we can prepare for midlife.

If you have always supported your husband's dreams, he will be less likely to regret the chances he never took or feel the need to leave his family to pursue unfulfilled longings in midlife. If you have been critical of his crazy ideas (a dream squasher), you may need to make a conscious effort to support him now. And he should be doing the same for you. Old patterns will no longer work when our dreams are at odds with each other.

The Stuff of Marriage

I am actually grateful to my crazy husband who has pushed me beyond my comfort zone. I have seen things and been exposed to experiences I never would have chosen. I have eaten bugs in the Australian rain forest (though I refused to eat iguana in Bonaire); I have done wheelies with my husband on a jet ski in the middle of the ocean; I have petted sting rays in the Great Barrier Reef (as my husband pointed out the lurking barracudas). I am even more thankful that he has infected our children with this enthusiasm for life and new experiences. Today they are adventurous young adults like their dad, thriving on travel, recreational sports, and new experiences, and I am thrilled for them. If I had raised my children alone, I would have been tempted to keep them within the four walls of our home so I could guarantee their safety. My husband would tell you that my methods may be safe, but they do not qualify as living. I would have raised three fearful, timid children.

My husband calls me his stubborn little donkey, digging in my heels at the first sight of change. I call him "hurricane man" or a human locomotive, barreling down the tracks. He says I'm too negative. I say that I am a realist, simply pointing out that he cannot be in four places at the same time. This is the stuff of marriage, whether we are in our twenties, our midlife years, or our eighties. Our goal is to make it through a lifetime of challenges and changes together.

Marriage is foremost a vocation. Two people are called together to fulfill the mission that God has given them.

Henri Nouwen

Guidance from God's Word

Adultery and the desire to find a new lover and partner are not new problems. These verses apply to both men and women who are tempted. We are encouraged (no, commanded) to find joy with the husband or wife we married in our youth.

Drink the water from your own cistern,
fresh water from your own well.
Do not let your fountains flow to waste elsewhere,
nor your streams in the public streets.
Let them be for yourself alone,
not for strangers at the same time.
And may your fountainhead be blessed!

Find joy with the wife you married in your youth,
fair as a hind, graceful as a fawn.
Let hers be the company you keep;
hers the breasts that ever fill you with delight,
hers the love that ever holds you captive.
Why be seduced, my son, by an alien woman,
and fondle the breast of a woman who is a stranger?
For the eyes of Yahweh observe a man's ways
and survey all his paths.
The wicked man is snared in his own misdeeds,
is caught in the meshes of his own sin.
For want of discipline, he dies,
and is lost through his own excessive folly.

PROVERBS 5:15–23

A harlot can be bought for a hunk of bread,
but the adulteress is aiming to catch a precious life.
Can a man hug fire to his breast
without setting his clothes alight?
Can a man walk on red-hot coals
without burning his feet?
So it is the man who consorts with his neighbor's wife:
no one who touches her will go unpunished.

PROVERBS 6:26–29

To turn from evil is the way of honest men;
he keeps his life safe who watches where he goes.

PROVERBS 16:17

A good wife, her husband's crown,
a shameless wife, a cancer in his bones.

PROVERBS 12:4

Questions
for Journaling and Discussion

1. How long have you been married? How did you meet your mate? What first attracted you to him?

2. How would you rate your marriage relationship on the compatibility scale? Do you view your differences as complementary, balancing one another, or conflictual? How do you each cope with change?

3. Which pitfalls do you relate to? Where is your relationship vulnerable?

4. Read Proverbs 7:18–23 and review the above verses. Have you known midlife men and women who were led to the slaughterhouse, unknowingly risking their lives? Can we play with fire and not get burned?

5. Extramarital affairs come in different forms (sexual and emotional). Some women feel that mistresses can also come in the form of consuming hobbies (e.g. sports). How can we be involved in other relationships and activities without robbing our marriages of the attention they deserve?

6. What are your midlife dreams? Your spouse's dreams? How can you support one another and find common ground?

Eccentricities and peculiarities you find charming in your courtship might drive you crazy one day, but if divorce is not part of your vocabulary, you'll learn to work through those things or even laugh them off. How much better to enjoy the differences and see the humor in them than to go berserk trying to change your partner!

Jerry Jenkins

The value of marriage is not that adults produce children, but that children produce adults.

Peter DeVries

Married couples are apt to find themselves in middle age, high and dry in an outmoded shell, in a fortress, which has outlived its function. What is one to do—die of atrophy in an outstripped form? Or move on to another form, other experiences?

Anne Morrow Lindbergh

Marriage with the long view comes with the conviction that nothing will break us up . . . this kind of commitment is not made just once, but over and over through the course of a lifetime. We cling to it during the dark nights of the soul that come to nearly every marriage, times when the love is hard to feel but the promise keeps us together.

William Doherty

Midlife Glimpses

After their youngest child left for college, Renee and Kevin celebrated their twenty-fifth wedding anniversary by traveling to Hawaii and renewing their wedding vows. They wanted to remember that their lives began without children at the center of their relationship. They intentionally marked the start of a new life together.

Tom and Sandy's last child left for college last year, and their dog recently died. Sandy is working full time and attending graduate courses at night. When Tom comes home from work, the house is quiet and he eats dinner by himself. Tom wonders if this lonely life is what midlife holds for him.

Jenny loved being a mom. Her husband traveled for a living and was often inattentive, but her children filled the void. When their last child left for college, Jenny began taking tennis lessons and spending time with her coach, an attractive man who took an interest in her. Jenny became even more aware of her empty marriage. She never intended to have an actual affair, but she had to admit that she was definitely emotionally involved with another man.

"Marriage is not a 50/50 arrangement. Each party must give 100 percent." This may be a popular saying about marriage, yet it's true that solid marriages have an equal amount of give and take. Mary Ann says that other friends may view her marriage as unhealthy, but she and her husband, Ron, are finding the empty nest years to be their best yet, due to patterns they established earlier in their marriage. They have always made a conscious effort to equally share everything in their lives (time, money, activities, chores, etc.). They do not engage in activities that separate them. When their children were involved in the high school band, Mary Ann and Ron were co-presidents of the band booster organization. Mary Ann regularly worked in the schools that her children attended. Today Ron and Mary Ann attend Bible studies together or weekend marriage retreats. They travel on vacations. They go for walks or out for coffee at the end of the day after work. Ron accompanies Mary Ann on shopping trips and she participates in his music activities. If Ron makes a large purchase for himself, he offers a proportionate amount of money for Mary Ann to buy something she would enjoy. Soon after both their children left for college, Mary Ann's mother developed dementia and died a year later. Through this difficult time of multiple losses, Mary Ann credits her husband with being her unfailing source of support.

Sue and Tom both have demanding jobs with long commutes. Sue loves her new midlife career and the opportunity to immerse herself in challenging tasks without the time constraints of motherhood. Sue and Tom are both contributing to the college tuition costs for their three children. They emotionally connect on the weekends and find they have interesting conversations about their busy weeks. Sometimes Tom sends Sue a bouquet of flowers to her office. They almost feel like they are dating again and enjoy the romance.

Leslie had always focused on her career. She thought that she and her husband had made a mutual decision not to have children. In midlife, Leslie's husband met someone else, married her, and started a family. Leslie did not realize how serious an issue she had put on hold until it was too late.

~

Cynthia and Roger blended their families when they married. Cynthia had three children from her first marriage, while Roger had joint custody of two children from a previous marriage. Their lives seemed to be a constant balancing act. After their last child left home, Cynthia and Roger experienced the honeymoon phase of marriage for the first time. They appreciated being alone together as a couple and made a conscious decision not to pursue hobbies or activities that they couldn't do together.

~

Debbie received her graduate degree in marine biology before staying home to raise two children. She worked in the local schools and at church as a dedicated volunteer. With their two children away at college, she and her husband are enjoying an unusually happy empty nest season. She credits this with their decision to spend time alone together as their children were growing up. They often took weekend trips or at least went out to dinner or to a movie one night a week. They also took family vacations to build memories as a family. Debbie's relationship with her husband was strong when their children left home. They celebrate the empty nest stage as an opportunity to spend even more time together, without the constraint of their children's busy schedules. Now they travel on longer trips, stopping to visit their children at their college campuses. Debbie viewed the first empty nest year as a transition year, not wanting to make hasty decisions about the future. She accepted more responsibilities in church leadership. The second year, she added working part-time at her husband's business. Debbie and her husband also made an effort to become more actively involved with their neighbors. Debbie believes that a vital marriage is the key to happiness in the empty nest years and must be established years before the children leave home.

Tina had been in an emotionally abusive marriage for twenty-five years. She tried everything to make their marriage work, not wanting her children to grow up in a fractured home like she had experienced as a child. She and her husband had been through counseling together. When her children began leaving home, Tina received training for a good job and was finally able to separate from her abusive husband.

During the 1970s, Jim Conway and his wife, Sally, assumed that their Christian faith and commitment to church would shield them from a midlife crisis. Jim, a minister and psychologist, was blindsided by his midlife meltdown. Jim and Sally began using their struggles to help other people. They started researching the topic, writing revolutionary books about the male midlife crisis, and giving workshops around the country.

During their only child's senior year in high school, Marian's husband died of cancer. When her child left home, she moved to a beach community she had always vacationed in, started working at an interesting job, and began a new life.

Cathy and Robert both grew up in the church and were committed Christians. They met in high school, married, and had two children. Cathy worked as the church secretary, and Robert was chairman of the deacon board. They were both involved in the church music program. Robert was a dedicated Boy Scout leader, often taking his son on scouting trips. In his midforties, Robert told Cathy that he wanted to leave. She begged him to stay and work on their marriage. She wanted them to seek counseling, but Robert refused. Cathy prayed for a miracle. Robert remained for a year (a tense, miserable year) and then one Saturday morning, as Cathy was reading her Bible, Robert packed his bags and left. Cathy later learned that Robert had had an affair a couple of years earlier. He moved home with his parents and has lived there for eleven years. Cathy did not file for divorce for a long time, hoping that Robert would recover from his midlife trauma and reconcile. Today they are divorced, and Cathy's greatest concern is for her adult children. Her son is thirty, living with her, and her daughter is twenty-seven years old. Neither of them have ever been in a serious relationship and she wonders how her husband's actions during their formative adolescence affected them.

Melanie's only child was a senior in high school, preparing to leave for college in another state. Melanie returned home one day to find a note from her husband, explaining that he was leaving her. All his clothes were gone. Melanie and her husband had attended church and sung in the choir together. Melanie was a dedicated Bible study teacher and speaker at women's retreats. She never saw her husband's departure coming. Melanie confronted her husband about another woman and he denied it. She soon learned that he had been lying and was involved with someone else. Melanie's chest pains were so severe that she went to her doctor for help. She was in a state of shock. Though Melanie's cardiac tests were normal, she was truly experiencing a broken heart.

Christi did not expect to be facing the empty nest at the young age of forty-two. She had married her husband, Ken, at age nineteen and was a mother by the time she turned twenty-one. When their last child left for college, they realized that they had to pioneer a new life. An adventurous soul by nature, Christi had put many of her dreams on hold to be a devoted mother. Ken had often traveled in his career. They had faced challenges in their marriage, sometimes feeling like ships passing in the night.

Christi encouraged her daughters to pursue their dreams,

travel, and receive an education before marriage. In midlife, Christi continued working at her daughters' former elementary school to help pay college tuitions but began to pursue some of her own dreams of the past. She and her husband made time to invest in a friendship. They started playing tennis together, read book club selections aloud to each other and discussed them, attended French classes at a local college, joined a wine tasting group that toured the Napa Valley, spent weekend retreats at a favorite beachside bed and breakfast inn, and even started making regular trips to France. They enjoyed visiting their youngest daughter who was studying abroad in Paris for one year. They are now preparing for a bike tour through Provence. As Ken showed genuine interest (not simply tolerance) and joined Christi in her pursuits, she made a decision to share his passion for baseball, frequently attending games with him. They have found their midlife relationship to be the best yet.

Cyndi and Dan longed for peace and quiet when they had teenagers at home. But when both children went off to college, they found their home to be too quiet. Six months before retirement, Dan underwent surgery for thyroid cancer. Though the tumor was precancerous, thyroid treatments caused Dan to spiral into a deep depression. After an exciting thirty-three-year career in law enforcement, Dan felt adrift. Cyndi continued working part-time, as Dan supported her by helping with household chores. They began traveling to foreign countries and discovered compatible hobbies. The city police department then offered Dan the position of Police Chaplain. Dan invited Cyndi to join him as co-chaplain, and they began training for crisis work together. Cyndi left her thirty-two-year career in the dental field to minister to the community. Once through the midlife transition, Dan and Cyndi found their empty nest years to be the most enjoyable yet, only outdone by the birth of their first grandchild.

~

Penny was curious why her neighbor, who had impeccable taste, was having her house painted a deep burgundy, so deep it would be difficult to ever paint over. When Penny visited her, she realized that the house was being painted that color inside and out. Her neighbor explained that her husband was leaving her for a younger woman and he would be receiving the house in the divorce settlement.

Chapter 8
Developing Midlife Support Networks

Brother helped by brother is a fortress,
friends are like the bars of a keep.
—Proverbs 18:19

In this time of our lives when we most need to feel part of a supportive community, midlife women often feel isolated and alone. Friends who were a regular part of our daily lives through our children's mutual activities are now moving in other directions. Our paths once naturally crossed while attending games, concerts, fund-raisers, school events, and more. We raised our children together over years, and now the glue is gone. We have every intention of remaining close, but the reality is that life has changed—including opportunities to gather together.

This transition may be especially difficult for "empty nest moms in process," those whose older children have left home but still have a younger child to raise. I attended school functions and band meetings for years with a close friend. Our daughters were like sisters. We had carpooled together since our daughters were in first grade and shared all the ups and downs of raising teenage girls. We talked weekly, working out schedule logistics. After our daughters left for college, I attended a band meeting for my younger son and realized that I no longer had my friend beside me. We stay in touch, try to meet for lunch once in a while, but I have to adjust to the fact that she is now working full-time in another city. With no children at home, her life has radically changed.

My friend Annie decided to build a new community of friends when she struggled with the isolation of the empty nest. She sent a letter to every empty nest mom she knew, asking if they'd be interested in forming a support group/Bible study for midlife moms. She was overwhelmed by the enthusiastic responses she received. The women felt the same way Annie did, but they didn't know how to reach out to one another. They now meet regularly to support one another and study God's Word.

A Sense of Community

Do you know that friendships are important to your health? A Harvard study found that the more friends a woman had, the healthier she was as she aged. Friendships add years to our lives. A physiological reason exists for why you seek comfort from other women when you are struggling. A UCLA study found that women under stress release the hormone *oxytocin.* (Testosterone increases in men experiencing stress.) Oxytocin buffers the "fight or flight" response to stress, instead encouraging us to nurture our children and relationships with other women. Oxytocin is enhanced by estrogen. The more we nurture relationships, the more oxytocin is released into our systems. Researchers found that oxytocin decreases stress and calms us. For centuries women have gathered together, turning to one another for support when the crises of life came.[1]

A sense of community is important as we age, especially when our children do not live nearby. No longer are empty nest couples downsizing and giving up their big family homes. I've recently read about a new trend among midlife couples preparing for retirement. These couples are building dream homes that are connected to one another, with some community areas or perhaps a pool, so they can live with their lifetime friends and continue a family support environment. They are also able to move to the mountains, desert, or beach resort areas, unaffected by the quality of the local school district. Empty nest does not necessarily have to mean a downsized, quiet lifestyle.

Supportive vs. Draining Relationships

It's time to take stock of your support networks. They will be critical to your adjustment to midlife changes. Think about your most important relationships with your spouse, children, parents, siblings, extended family, friends, co-workers, etc. Take a sheet of paper, draw a line down the middle, and write SUPPORTIVE on one side and DRAINING on the other side.

List your relationships in the most appropriate category. Joyce Landorf once labeled relationships as "balcony people" or "basement people." Balcony people cheer you on while basement people drag you down. Many of your familial relationships are probably supportive and draining at the same time. You can place them smack in the middle. Your husband can be your greatest supporter or saboteur, depending on how he adjusts to his midlife changes. We've been blessed in that my husband's parents and my mom are in their eighties and still unusually active, healthy, and independent. They are our role models for aging. They have remained young at heart, always learning new things and seeking new experiences. They are supportive of us and especially supportive of their grandchildren. Yet I realize that many midlife couples are dealing with failing parents and the heavy responsibility of caring for them. If we have lost a parent, we often take a more active role with our remaining parent who is now widowed.

Now take a second sheet of paper, again writing SUPPORTIVE and DRAINING on each side. This time think about how others perceive you. Are you supportive or draining? Perhaps you are a little of both. Now list your life relationships in the appropriate category, from the perspective of your spouse, children, parents, siblings, extended relatives, friends, co-workers, etc. How do they see you? If you are brave, you can ask these people how they view your relationship. It may surprise you.

It's time to compare the lists. Are the same people listed on both sheets of paper? Or are you supporting (or draining) someone who does not even count as a significant relationship on your sheet?

Now compare the categories. Are they the same lists on each sheet? Are you in mutually supportive relationships, mutually draining relationships, or one supports/one drains relationships? How many "smack in the middle" relationships do you have on each sheet? Are they the same on both?

Study the lists carefully, thinking about the impact on your life. These are your support networks. Healthy relationships are mutually supportive, even with bumps along the way. You are richly blessed if you have ten supportive relationships and one or two draining relationships.

During this stressful time of change, perhaps most of your relationships are smack in the middle. You may be struggling if you have ten draining relationships and one or two supportive relationships. Classic codependents have support/drain relationships. If you have no mutually supportive relationships, you may need to seriously consider that you need help learning to be supportive of others. Healthy, supportive people usually attract other healthy, supportive people.

Sometimes a timeline is helpful. Relationships can change over decades. What began as a healthy, supportive relationship may now be a draining relationship, and vice versa.

In the midst of your changing roles as a mother, daughter, and wife, the one role that doesn't need to change is your role as friend. Hopefully you have been investing in deep friendships throughout the past decades. They will be your lifeline now. The most important constant is your relationship with God.

Perhaps because I was raised as an only child, I have experienced unusually rich, deep, abiding friendships with other women. With a couple of exceptions, my closest friends do not have sisters. It's almost as if we were searching for surrogate sisters. These women are family to me. At every juncture of major change in my life, God sent a specific person to walk beside me—"Jesus with skin on." Usually an instant connection occurred that has endured to this day. I consider these friendships, which have lasted for decades through thick and thin, to be one of my greatest gifts in life.

As a midlife mom, these deep core relationships have not changed. Yet my peripheral friendships, relationships of mutual circumstances, have changed. My day-to-day world of sharing life with the parents of my children's friends has disappeared. Through the years, my children's activities at school, church, and in the community consistently provided me with ways to meet new people and make new friends. Now I must create my own opportunities.

Guidance from God's Word

Fragrant oil gladdens the heart,
friendship's sweetness comforts the soul.
Do not abandon friend, or father's friend;
when trouble comes, do not go running to your brother's house.
Better a friend near than a brother far away.

PROVERBS 27:9–10

Make the wise your companions and you grow wise yourself;
make fools your friends and suffer for it.
PROVERBS 13:20

Without deliberation plans come to nothing,
where counselors are many plans succeed.
PROVERBS 15:22

Questions
for Journaling and Discussion

1. Read Ecclesiastes 4:9–11, describing a mutually supportive relationship. Think of a mutually supportive relationship where you have helped each other up when the other has fallen.

2. Think of special friends and relatives who have:
   - gladdened your heart and comforted your soul.
   - wisely advised you and encouraged you to make wise decisions.

3. Have your opportunities to spend time with friends changed? How has your child's departure from home affected regularly seeing other parents? Write down some specific ways you can purposefully nurture friendships now that your paths do not naturally cross.

4. Brainstorm about ways to create your own empty nest support group, from meeting with three friends for coffee once a month to organizing a weekly church Bible study for a large group, perhaps using this book as a tool.

The hardest part of relationships is being in them.

Nicole Johnson

Friends are relatives you make for yourself.

Eustache DeChamps

A real friend deserves to know when you've failed, when you're feeling vulnerable, and when you are hanging by your fingernails, because that friend has invested emotionally in you.

The best thing about long-term friends is that they don't just hear about your past; they're part of it. That makes the relationship worth preserving.

Jerry Jenkins

Midlife Glimpses

Jodie was the first of her local girl friends to have all of her children off at college. She felt isolated as her friends remained busy parenting their younger children. Jodie was unprepared for the identity crisis and accompanying depression she experienced. She felt lost not being a mom on a daily basis and without the social connections that role provided. Jodie knew that she needed to take specific steps to face this new stage of life. She joined a local exercise program to increase her energy level and decrease depression. She began attending a women's Bible study at her church and immersed herself in God's Word. As her friends' children began leaving home in the years to come, Jodie would meet her friends for outings. They developed an informal support group, encouraging one another and praying for their college students.

As a single parent, Abby had enjoyed her relationship with her only daughter. They were mother and daughter, yet they were buddies too. When her daughter left for college, Abby was unusually lonely and needed the support of friends to help her cope. One friend made a point of meeting Abby for dinner one night every week.

Susan and Kathryn had been close friends ever since their firstborn children were toddlers. When their last children left for college, Susan converted a large playhouse in the backyard into an art studio while Kathryn converted an extra bedroom into her office for a new business. Enjoying the process together, they started an informal support group for other mid-life moms, called "A Room of One's Own." Mothers met in a safe place to discuss their feelings of loss and to brainstorm future possibilities.

Chapter 9
Developing Friendships With Your Adult Children

You paved the road for me, but let me make my own journey.
—Virginia Reynolds

Cultivating friendships with your adult children is one of your most important midlife goals. We have not *lost* a child but gained the unique opportunity to develop a mutually supportive relationship. This process doesn't happen overnight. You will not enjoy a true adult friendship with your children until they are financially and emotionally independent, but you are laying the foundation now.

Ideally you began laying that foundation in their childhood. My husband and I have always felt blessed that we not only love our children, but we like them. They are funny, bright, interesting people, and we would rather spend time with them than with anyone else. We would rather vacation with them than with any other friends. I would rather plan a fun family dinner for my children than an elegant dinner party for my peers. My husband and I tried to keep in mind that we were raising children who would become adults that we would want as a part of our lives. We were building a future support network. Hopefully they will support one another as adult siblings when we are gone. As one mother shared with me, "The most important gift you can give your children is to communicate that you truly enjoy them and would choose their company."

Five Basic Rules

Lord, please help me to remember to treat my children as You treat me . . . with love, grace, and lots of mercy.

Gigi Graham Tchividjian

Here are five basic rules for developing friendships with adult children that I have gleaned from other mothers:

Rule #1—Listen more than you talk.

Rule #2—Offer a safe, confidential place for them to share without fear of judgment.

Rule #3—Do not give unasked-for advice (unless your child is truly in danger). Wait for your child to ask for your input. If your child never asks, and you just can't keep quiet any longer, you might say, "Would you like my opinion on that situation?" But then respect their wishes.

Rule #4—Speak to them with the same courtesy you would use in speaking to a close friend. For example, you would not greet a close friend with, "Why don't you do something with your hair? You're not really going to wear that, are you? Have you gained weight?"

Rule #5—Look for fun opportunities to contact your children. Never make them feel guilty for not contacting you first. Always be thrilled to hear from them when they do call or write.

Staying Involved

Life is the first gift, love is the second, and understanding the third.
Margie Piercy

The good news for empty nest parents is that we can be as involved as we want in our children's lives, completely independent of their need to contact us. Many empty nest parents are surprised and saddened by the initial lack of contact. They are upset when their children call only when they need money.

Our children have new lives, new friends, and new support systems. We have prepared them for this adventure. They still need our love and support. Our challenge is communicating that love in creative, not intrusive, ways.

Here are some of the best ideas I have learned from observing other empty nest moms:

Care packages remain the best way to send "love in a box" to college students, filled with needed items, their favorite foods, silly cards, family photos of recent events, local newspaper clippings, letters from siblings, and more.

One mom scouted out all the eateries and stores near her son's college campus during their orientation weekend. Throughout the year, she sent him gift certificates to those places.

Another mom rises early every morning to e-mail greetings to her college-age daughters. She updates them on family news, includes Bible verses or meaningful quotes, and asks them what she can be praying for that day.

Some mothers' groups have gathered to pray for their children ever since they attended grade school. College-age children need prayer now more than ever. Some empty nest moms gather to support one another and continue praying for their children at their respective colleges.

One couple videotaped the family happenings during the month and sent a video to their firstborn child who was attending college across the country. It always arrived on the first of the month. Another mom tape-recorded their family's Sunday dinner conversation and weekly sent it to her daughter. Sometimes they would talk to her on the tape as if she was at the table with them.

Finals snack baskets, whether you personally prepare them or send them through a school program, are a great way to encourage your child during the stressful week of finals. Midterm time is another good opportunity for sending some extra energy and encouragement.

Some parents make an effort to visit their student once each month, taking their child and his or her friends out to a favorite local restaurant.

Some moms enjoy sending treats for their college student to open on each day of the week. For example, for one daughter's birthday week, her mom sent streamers on Monday, a birthday banner on Tuesday, napkins and plates on Wednesday, and a gift certificate for an ice-cream cake from Baskin-Robbins on Thursday. A balloon bouquet arrived on Friday, her eighteenth birthday. Another creative mom sent graham crackers on Monday, candy bars on Tuesday, and marshmallows on Wednesday, so her son could make s'mores on the weekend. Some parents like their children to receive daily mail while others like to send a large package with the wrapped treats labeled "Open on Monday," etc.

On her daughter's first birthday away from home, one mom created a computer Web page, where all their friends and relatives could send birthday greetings and fun photos.

One father wrote to his son every day when his son joined the military. From personal experience, the father knew how important it was that his son daily receive a letter of encouragement.

Many parents try to attend any special events that their student is participating in, such as concerts, plays, or sporting events, celebrating their child's recent achievements.

One couple annually vacations near their children's college campuses. They rent a condominium on the ocean, equidistant from the two colleges, for two weeks. Their son and daughter visit them during the evenings and on weekends. This arrangement brings a touch of home to the students and provides a break from their stressful studies. The parents enjoy a relaxing vacation at the beach as well as time together as a family.

When her children return home on breaks, one mother treats them as her favorite visitors and honored guests, pampering them with their favorite foods and activities. She wants her children to view home as a welcome retreat from the pressures of school.

Continue to include your college-age child in all of your regular family traditions, such as celebrating holidays or special family times. Look for ways to include them by phone or by sending tokens for the celebrations. Make them feel that they remain part of the family.

Be sensitive to your child's new life and schedule, never possessive or demanding of his or her time. Our daughter's birthday occurred three weeks after she left for her freshman year. She didn't know one person at her new college and was miles away from home, so we planned a surprise birthday visit. Fortunately, we decided to warn her that we were coming to celebrate her birthday. She kindly told us that she already had birthday plans with all of her new "best friends" and would be away on a weekend retreat. We told her that we were thrilled she was so happy in her new environment. Our goal as parents is to continue making our children feel special, never guilty.

Veteran moms agree that new empty nest moms should make plans to treat themselves, in addition to sending treats to their new college students. Plan a special trip with your husband or a luncheon event with friends. Splurge on a spa day. Take a class or try a new hobby. Pamper yourself. Have something to look forward to as soon as possible after your child leaves for school.

The Room Issue

Silent messages speak volumes to young people. Parents are often tempted to immediately turn their child's empty room into an office, guest bedroom, sewing room, or other coveted space. This may help parents bring closure to their grief as they transition into the empty nest years, but it doesn't help their children. Most young people feel displaced when they lose their rooms at home or when their parents move into a smaller new house. Our children possess the courage to go out into the world because their roots at home are secure. They need somewhere safe and familiar to return to.

If possible, wait until your child is established in his or her new world before making major changes in your lifestyle. This may take a few months for some children or a few years for others. You don't want to communicate that your child no longer has a place in your home or family. You shouldn't put your life on hold indefinitely, but be aware of your child's individual needs.

Why Letting Go of Our Children Helps Them

> *Every word and deed of a parent is a fiber woven into the character of a child that ultimately determines how that child fits into the fabric of society.*
>
> David Wilkerson

While we can ease our children into adulthood with sensitivity by keeping their rooms intact, sending care packages, and planning special family events, we still must let go of our full-time parenting role for their sakes.

Our generation is the first one to over-invest in our children's lives, often hindering their growth toward independence. This recent development in society is called "perma-parenting." It's defined as continuing to parent adult children, being invested in their lives' successes and failures when no longer appropriate. In her book *When Our Grown Kids Disappoint Us,* Jane Adams says that parents naturally expect a return on their investment of raising children, wanting them to be productive, happy, independent adult members of society. When this doesn't occur, parents compensate with *more* parenting, bailing children out financially and emotionally. This vicious cycle becomes harder and harder to break.

Rarely did an adult child live with parents in our parents' or grandparents' generation. Today it is not unusual for thirty-year-old children to remain living at home or return home after a divorce or job loss.

Linda allowed her twenty-nine-year-old son to return home

after his job was terminated. He was in debt to credit card companies and his wife had left him. Linda wanted to be supportive, unconditionally love her son, and help him get back on his feet. He agreed to pay rent to her as soon as he secured new employment and move out within six months. Yet the weeks turned into months, and the months turned into years. Linda's son couldn't keep a job more than a few months. Instead of helping her financially, he began to borrow money from her to pay his bills. Linda couldn't break the cycle.

Moms and dads who won't let go of their parenting role or allow their adult children to cling to them in unhealthy ways can cripple them. Embracing the empty nest stage may be the best thing you do for your young adult child.

Encouragement from God's Word

The crown of the aged is their children's children;
the children's glory is their father.
PROVERBS 17:6

White hairs are a crown of honor,
they are found in the paths of virtue.
PROVERBS 16:31

As you make this transition to becoming adult friends with your children and someday perhaps having grandchildren in your lives, you cultivate healthy relationships that will become your crown.

Questions
for Journaling and Discussion

1. Which of the five basic rules did you find most challenging?

2. Brainstorm fun and creative ways to stay connected with your child.

3. Many empty nest parents feel that they are in a state of limbo—wanting to start a new job, move to a new home or area, or make another major life change—yet they do not want their children to feel misplaced. Do you feel that your life is on hold? How can you benefit from this transition period?

4. Family experts say that having smaller families makes it more difficult for parents to let go of their children today. Reflect on the adage, "More is not necessarily better." Describe the difference between parenting and perma-parenting. Which parenting approach does the Bible encourage?

Every mother is like Moses. She does not enter the promised land. She prepares a world she will not see.

Pope Paul VI

The years with my children have taught me there is no such thing as quality time; there is only time, and if you spend enough of it, some of it turns out to be quality.

Karen Hughes

I do believe that life is a series of small choices through which we sometimes communicate big things.

Karen Hughes

Parenthood is a partnership with God . . . you are working with the Creator of the universe in shaping human character and determining destiny.

Ruth Vaughn

Lord, send a guardian angel to watch over their going out and their coming in, and lead them not into temptation, but deliver them from the evil one. Send enough rain to keep them dependent on You but enough sun to give them hope and encouragement. And, Lord, when they're standing at the crossroads trying to decide which path to take, put a person of faith there to point them in the right direction.

Shirley Dobson

"A Mother's Prayer"[1]

Chapter 10
The Midlife Miracle

And now I send an angel before you to guard you on your way and to bring you to the place I have prepared.

—Exodus 23:20

In the midst of our midlife struggles, we as Christians have the unique privilege to gain something that surpasses all our losses. We begin to experience some spiritual maturity, which will potentially ripen into wisdom.

My eldest daughter works during the summers to pay for her personal expenses for the school year. This past summer she lost her job in mid-July. Distraught, she didn't know how she would pay her car insurance and other bills in the coming year. Within forty-eight hours, through miraculous circumstances, she had a new and better job, which she could continue part-time through the year. God's intervention was clearly evident to her, and her faith was buoyed.

God's provision in my daughter's situation brought back memories from my early twenties. I was a relatively new Christian and God's hand was evident at every turn in my life. I remember experiencing miracle after miracle of His guidance and intervention. I have often observed that God is especially encouraging with young believers, whether young in chronological years or young in coming to faith in Jesus Christ. In our early development, God gives us tangible markers to affirm our trust in His care and sovereign power over our lives.

In my thirties I began to wonder why the more tangible miracles were drying up. When I was struggling, why didn't God simply change the circumstances? I knew He could. Why didn't He open the door to new opportunities? Why didn't He close the door on old problems? God was weaning me off milk to take solid food. He was beginning His course in building spiritual character. He was no longer changing my life circumstances. Now God wanted to change *me*.

His Miraculous Presence

By listening to God through His Word, I began to glimpse a deeper miracle. God rarely delivered those He loved most from suffering, nor did He miraculously change their circumstances. Paul was shipwrecked and imprisoned, his life fraught with problems. Not even God's beloved Son was exempt.

The greater miracle was the gift of God's presence and protection in the midst of suffering. Contrast the experience of believers in Hebrews 11:32–35 with Hebrews 11:35–40. The faith described in Hebrews 11:32–35 has been called "Noah faith." These men were delivered *from* suffering. The faith described in Hebrews 11:35–40 has been called "Job faith." These men who were called to die for their faith were delivered *through* suffering.

Shadrach, Meshach, and Abednego were bound and thrown into a fiery furnace, heated to seven times its normal heat. The guards who threw them into the furnace were even killed by the flames. King Nebuchadnezzar was amazed to see a "fourth man" in the furnace. Shadrach, Meshach, and Abednego emerged from the inferno unharmed, not a single hair on their heads singed.

Daniel was thrown into the lion pit. God sent an angel to seal the lions' jaws. Yet when Daniel's accusers and their families were thrown into the lion pit, they were seized and crushed before they reached the ground.

God did not stop Shadrach, Meshach, and Abednego from being thrown in the furnace or Daniel from being thrown in the lion pit. He went with them. Can you imagine how terrified they were?

Storms of Life

As the wife of a man who loves boats and the ocean, I have been quite seasick and scared during some of our trips. I can relate to the disciples who feared storms. In Mark 4:37–41 Jesus sleeps on a cushion in the boat during a storm, where waves are nearly swamping the boat. The disciples finally wake him up, asking Jesus, "Don't you care if we drown?" Then Jesus calms the storm but rebukes his followers, "Why are you so afraid? Have you still no faith?" Read Mark 6:45–51:

> *Immediately Jesus made his disciples get into the boat and go on ahead of him to Bethsaida, while he dismissed the crowd. After leaving them, he went up on a mountainside to pray.*
>
> *When evening came, the boat was in the middle of the lake, and he was alone on land. He saw the disciples straining at the oars, because the wind was against them. About the fourth watch of the night he went out to them. He was about to pass by them, but when they saw him walking on the lake, they thought he was a ghost. They cried out, because they all saw him and were terrified.*
>
> *Immediately he spoke to them and said, "Take courage! It is I. Don't be afraid." Then he climbed into the boat with them, and the wind died down.*

Jesus watched His disciples struggle until the fourth watch. He could have calmed the wind from shore at any time. But Jesus waited. Then He went out to be with His friends in their struggle. God's relationship with us and our trust in Him are more important than any immediate solution to an earthly problem. God comforts us with His presence, saying, "Take courage! It is I. Don't be afraid."

The identifying mark of a believer on the road to spiritual maturity, hopefully by midlife, is an understanding of the miracle of God's presence. We experience an unswerving trust in God no matter how desperate life's circumstances appear. In our twenties most of us do not have enough life experience or have not journeyed long enough with God to comprehend this. We can't see the big picture. Spiritual perspective is a bonus of the midlife years.

Perhaps on some days you feel like you've been thrown to the lions or in a fiery furnace. You may be experiencing more Job days than Noah days. You may feel that your life has been shipwrecked or, at least, the waves are swamping the boat. You are tired of rowing against the wind without a break. Like the disciples, you may cry out, "Lord, don't you care if I drown?"

He cares. In the midst of all our midlife losses, God cares. He hasn't left your side.

Take courage. It is I. Don't be afraid.

Comfort from God's Word

That is why each of your servants prays to you
in time of trouble;
even if floods come rushing down,
they will never reach him.
You are a hiding place for me,
you guard me when in trouble.
You surround me with songs of deliverance.
PSALM 32:6–7

I need only say, "I am slipping,"
and your love, Yahweh, immediately supports me;
and in the middle of all my troubles
you console me and make me happy.
PSALM 94:18–19

Questions
for Journaling or Discussion

1. Think of a specific time in your life when:
   - God allowed the storm in your life to continue for an extended period.
   - you trusted God when earthly circumstances looked hopeless.
   - God guarded you on your way and brought you to a place He prepared (Exodus 23:20).
2. In those times, how did God reveal His presence to you?

Difficulty is actually the atmosphere surrounding a miracle, or a miracle in its initial stage. Yet if it is to be a great miracle, the surrounding condition will be not simply a difficulty but an utter impossibility. And it is the clinging hand of His child that makes a desperate situation a delight to God.

L. B. Cowman

In the darkness of the tunnel, merely "keeping on" becomes a miracle.

Verdell Davis

Chapter 11
Traveling Through the Valley

You may let me out of your sight, but never out of your heart.
—Virginia Reynolds

"Now that I have time to prepare all those great home-cooked meals, I don't have anyone left at home to cook for." My friend remarks. Our flip-flopped lives seem ironic. All the things we said we would do if we had more time no longer seem relevant.

Through my office window I can see our neighbors' backyard, filled with a sandbox, trampoline, slides, swings, wading pool, and other equipment to entertain young children. While I write, I can see and hear their children playing and laughing. I remember when my backyard was filled with similar toys and our children were laughing and playing. Sometimes I want to go back in time just for a single day, to hold my young children, play with them, and know they are completely safe because I never let them out of my sight.

The 9/11 terrorist attack occurred two weeks after my eldest left for college. She lived in a target city. Intellectually I knew that God kept her eternally safe, no matter where she lived. Yet I felt helpless to protect her. I knew that keeping my children within sight was only an illusion of safety. Since then, my daughter has attended school abroad and traveled throughout Europe. As my adventurous husband keeps reminding me, "Ships are safe in the harbor, but that's not what ships are for."

Parenting is a continual process of letting go more and more.

Next to Jesus Christ, my family has been the earthly center of my world. This experience is a double-edged sword. The more time we spent with our children, the more available we were, and the more immersed we were in their lives, the more difficult is our separation from them and the bigger the hole they leave. My children did not cross the Atlantic Ocean, but I experienced my own "bowl of tears." On bad days, I felt like all the sunshine had gone out of my life. Today I am overwhelmed with gratefulness that God allowed me the privilege of not missing one minute with my children. I could never get that time back.

We drove our second daughter to college this fall to begin her freshman year. I thought her departure would be easier than my first experience, since she selected a college closer to home and I had already gone through this experience once before. Of course, I was wrong. It was just as hard, perhaps harder. Now both my daughters are gone. My husband's life continues to become busier. He copes with loss differently than I do. He is immersed in two separate careers, traveling for both.

When my son entered high school this year, I realized in a panic—approaching sheer terror—that in a few years my husband and I would probably be driving him to college ... and then what? I would return to an empty house—empty of children yet full of memories.

Even with all the preparation I had done to avoid one, I was forty-nine years old and having a midlife meltdown. I remembered my friend's words. I had interviewed her because I observed that she had done everything right in managing her midlife transition. Yet she shared with me:

> *While the exterior of my life has everything in place to prevent a midlife meltdown, the reality is that the activities themselves haven't prevented one. I am currently in the biggest funk of my life. I've hit a*

new low searching for purpose, meaning in life, unfulfilled dreams, etc. The depression that I've struggled with all of my life has become much more pronounced. I try to remember that midlife is a phase, like our children's "terrible twos" or teenage years, for reevaluating who I am today and who God is asking me to become. It's not so terrifying to walk in this dark place if I know it's only a valley and not an alley.

No matter how we prepare for it, traveling through this valley is inevitable for every midlife woman, especially for devoted mothers separating from their children. But we are not trapped in a dead end alley. The gift of midlife is the ability to recognize God's track record. We remember every time God faithfully sustained us when we had lost hope in the future. We remember the surprises He had in store for us when the enemy of our souls whispered, "This time God has forgotten you." We know that God is smiling as He walks through the valley with us . . . because He has lovingly planned what awaits us next.

But I will court her again and bring her into the wilderness, and speak to her tenderly there. There I will give back her vineyards to her and transform her Valley of Troubles into a Door of Hope.

HOSEA 2:14–15A

THE LIVING BIBLE

Mezpah—

A biblical word meaning:
The Lord watch between thee and me
while we are away one from the other.

Mother's Covers

When you were small
And just a touch away,
I covered you with blankets
Against the cool night air.

But now that you are tall
And out of reach
I fold my hands
And cover you with prayer.

Unknown

Ten Steps to Avoiding a Midlife Meltdown

1. Mourn the loss of a daily relationship with your child. Allow yourself to grieve.
2. Identify each change and stressor that you are experiencing this year. Face challenges or unresolved issues in your other relationships head on.
3. Focus on God's Word and His eternal purpose vs. the external goals prevalent in our culture. Invest time developing inner beauty vs. outer beauty.
4. Make peace with the roles you have chosen through different seasons of life, and be open to exploring new opportunities. Become proactive, not reactive. Be willing to take risks, knowing that God goes before you to plan the way and He comes behind to hold you up (Isaiah 52:12).
5. Find meaningful ways to give back to the next generation. Look for opportunities to be a mentor.
6. Celebrate the treasure that has been buried in your own backyard. Discover ways that your children have prepared you to enter this new life stage.
7. Identify challenges and vulnerable areas in your midlife marriage. Invest time in developing a friendship, supporting one another's dreams and goals. Make an effort to find

common ground when your plans collide. Be patient with one another, realizing that each partner copes with change and loss in different ways.

8. Develop mutually supportive relationships, within and outside your family. Identify your lifeline, your core support network of friends and relatives. Ideally build an informal support group of other midlife moms facing the empty nest transition.
9. Appreciate that the midlife season has gifted you with the roots of spiritual maturity and wisdom. Immerse yourself in God's Word, seeking Him with your whole heart. Consciously remember God's track record in your life, especially during difficult experiences.
10. Cultivate friendships with your adult children. Be understanding of their rapidly changing lives and remain their anchor at home. Find creative, fun ways to connect with your children.

Enjoy your midlife masterpiece.

Endnotes

Chapter 2

1. Viorst, Judith. *Necessary Losses.* Ballantine Books, 1986.

Chapter 3

1. Rosemond, John. "Self-respect should be the goal of child-rearing." *Contra Costa Times.*

Chapter 5

1. Lindbergh, Anne Morrow. *Gift From the Sea.* Pantheon Books, 1955.

Chapter 6

1. Paterson, Katherine. *A Sense of Wonder.* Penguin Books, 1995.
2. Graglia, F. Carolyn. *Domestic Tranquility: A Brief Against Feminism.* Spence Publishing, 1998.

Chapter 8

1. Courter, Gay and Pat Gaudette. *How to Survive Your Husband's Midlife Crisis.* Perigee Publishers, 2003.

Chapter 9

1. "A Mother's Prayer," poem by Shirley Dobson. Graham, Ruth Bell. *Prayers from a Mother's Heart.* Thomas Nelson Publishers, 1999.